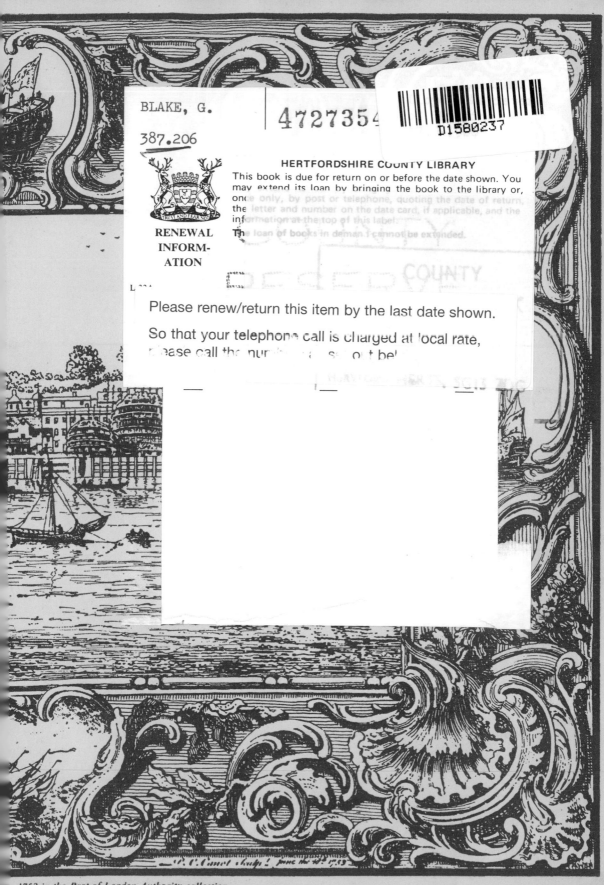

n 1753 in the Port of London Authority collection

LLOYD'S REGISTER OF SHIPPING

1760-1960

The Arms granted to Lloyd's Register of Shipping in 1958

LLOYD'S REGISTER
OF SHIPPING
1760-1960

by George Blake

Illustrated by David Knight, M.S.I.A.

PRINTED IN GREAT BRITAIN BY LLOYD'S REGISTER OF SHIPPING AT GARRETT HOUSE, MANOR ROYAL, CRAWLEY, SUSSEX.

CONTENTS

ILLUSTRATIONS

INTRODUCTION

This is the story of an enterprise which began 200 years ago in Edward Lloyd's Coffee House in the City of London. It must not be confused with the great insurance house, the Corporation of Lloyd's, which also came into existence in the same coffee house. Each organisation went its own way: the one dealing with insurance and the other with the classification of ships. The latter eventually became known as Lloyd's Register of Shipping.

I am glad that the story of Lloyd's Register of Shipping over 200 years has now been written. The development from the coffee house days is of much interest. This great organisation has played a notable part in the history of shipping throughout the world and has contributed to its well-being in peace and war.

During its 200 years the Society has seen the passing of the wooden ship under sail and the iron ship. It has witnessed the introduction of steam, the steel ship and the diesel engine and is now on the threshold of nuclear power for marine propulsion.

Lloyd's Register of Shipping is an international body dealing with ships of all nations. It has no capital, no shareholders, no articles of association; it pays no dividends. It only has one object: "impartial service". Its activities are controlled by a General Committee consisting of shipowners, underwriters, shipbuilders, enginebuilders and steelmakers drawn from many countries.

In the early days some 16 ex-captains acted as Surveyors. To-day there are over 1,000 technically qualified Surveyors distributed throughout the ports of the world, surveying ships and ancillary undertakings.

In later days the Society has developed a Land Division covering the survey of oil refineries, pipelines, thermal and hydro-electric power stations, wind tunnels and, now, installations equipped with nuclear reactors.

It is, indeed, a story of adventure by an organisation probably unique in the world: old in origin, progressive in outlook.

Chairman

A LIST of SHIPS that are Sail'd from *England*, for *East-India* and *China*, and that are not Return'd or known in *England* to Miscarry, and to whom they belong.

Note, O, stands for Old; E, for English Company, and P, for Private Trade.

	Ships Names.	Commanders Names.	Tons.	Guns.	Men.	Where Bound.	When Sail'd.
P	Buckhurft	——Penluce	380	40	60	Muscat	August 16. 1698.
E	Rook-Gally	George Simons	250	20	50	Surrat	Ditto 1699.
E	Limpoy	Thomas Monke	160	16	130	Stays in India	February 22.
E	Albermarle	William Beawes	350	28	65	Surrat	April 24. 1700.
O	Martha	Thomas Raines	600	40	80	Bombay	May 14.
O	Rebecca	Thomas Maflin	120	10	20	Malegafcar	June 25.
P	Borneo	Henry Berry	300	24	55	Borneo	July 4.
E	New Advife	——Redhead	160	16	36	Fort & Bay	6.
+ E	Rifing-Sun	Arthur Holford	140	13	27	China	November 1.
E	China-Merchant	Francis Hofier	170	14	35	Ditto	19.
E	Sarah-Gally	John Roberts	275	22	55	Ditto	Ditto
O	Hampfhire	Zachary Tovey	375	26	75	Fort St. George	December 27.
O	Bedford	John Hudfon	750	46	150	Ditto	22.
E	Bengall	Henry Trenwith	390	30	78	Coaft & Bay	January 5.
P	Eakins-Frigate	——Stettell					22.
O	Phœnix	Thomas Lambert	400	28	80	Bengall	Ditto
E	Degraves	William Young	520	36	104	Coaft & Bay	February 19.
+ P	Siphio	George Luke Burwich	400	26	70	Coaft of India	20.
O	Loyal Cooke	Richard Bolton	330	30	66	Maderas & China	March 3.
E	Sufannah	William Ingledew	350	24	70	Surrat	April 3. 1701.
E	Catharine	William Holeman	208	20	51	Bay	16.
E	Nathanael	Charles Hill	250	26	50	Surrat	20.
E	Rebow	Thomas Dennett	150	14	30	Ditto	Ditto
O	Loyal Blifs	Robert Hudfon	350	28	70	Bombay	May 30.
+ O	Hern-Frigate	John Lane	150	20	30	Ditto	June 29.
O	John & Mary	Bayly Kent	200	16	40	Bencola	July 15.
E	Upton-Gally	John Cammell	180	16	40	Surrat	August 3.
E	Macclesfield-Frigate	Thomas Roberts	312	30	60	Borneo	September 15.
O	Orenzebe	John Elewett	425	30	87	China	October 1.
P	Chambers-Frigate	Thomas South	350	30	72	Coaft of India	November 2.
P	Conftant Friend	John Lackey	220	22	44	Ditto	22.
+ P	Profperous	——Hilliard	220	20	40	Ditto	Ditto
E	Canterbury	Enock Kingsford	340	28	66	China	December 7.
E	Hallifax	Henry Hudfon	340	20	70	Ditto	Ditto
E	Arabia-Factor	Abram Jackfon	140	16	28	Mocho	Ditto
E	Union	John Palmer	208	20	40	China	January 1.
P	Robert & Nathanael	John Smith	230	20	46	Ditto	Ditto
+ E	Macclesfield-Gally	John Hurle	250	20	46	Ditto	Ditto
+ P	London	George Matthews	400	34	90	Borneo	March 5.
O	Pancher	Robert Robinfon	400	24	70	Ditto	Ditto
+ P	Frederick	John Winn	350	30	70		8.
+ E	Worcefter	Thomas Green	380	16	32	Ditto	
+ E	Tankervil	Charles Newnham	425	34	85	Coaft & Bay	Ditto
+ E	Union	John Goodfale	140	14	28	Amoy & China	Ditto
O	Wentworth	Thomas Sax	350	24	70	Ditto	Ditto
O	Fleet-Frigate	Thomas Burges	280	22	56	Cantoone	Ditto
E	Norris	James Alifon	600	36	118	Coaft & Bay	10.
O	Colchefter	Benjamin Roufe	500	36	90	Ditto	19.
O E	Edward & Dudley	William Lambert	300	24	60	Borneo	April 12. 1702.
+ E	Hern-Frigate	William Morris	250	20	50	Ditto	Ditto
+ O	Glocefter	Philip Browne	350	30	70	Bencola	August 15.
O	Regard	Thomas Warner	250	24	50	Surrat	Ditto
O	Howland-Frigate	Thomas Hayes	400	32	80	Ditto	Ditto
E	Mary	Chriftopher Liell	458	30	90	Ditto	27.
E	Catharine	James Junifer	495	30	99	Ditto	Ditto
E	Samuel & Anne	Finch Reddall	180	16	36	Borneo	September 1.
+ E	Refolution	William Doyley	300	26	60	Mocho	Ditto
+ P	Alexander-Gally	Joshuah Winter	—	—	—		Preparing to Sail.
+ P	Black Boy	——Penruddock	—	—	—		Preparing to Sail.

SHIPS Arriv'd from *East-India* and *China* fince the 23th of *December*, 1701.

	Ships Names.	Commanders Names.	Tons.	Guns.	Men.	From what Place.	When Arriv'd.
O	King William	John Braddyll	600	36	120	Fort St. George	February 2. 1701.
E	Mountague	John Collier	460	30	80	Surrat & Perfia	April 4. 1702.
O	Maderas	John Aprife	250	24	50	Bencola	Ditto
+ P	Mansell-Frigate	John Clarke	400	26	70	Ditto	June 11.
O	Duchefs	Hugh Raymond	450	28	91	Fort St. George	Ditto
O E	Julia	William Morris	260	18	50	Borneo	Ditto
E	Rifing-Eagle	Benjamin Boucher	150	16	40	Bengall	July 7.
E	Difcovery	John Evans	208	16	42	Mocho	21.
+ E	Trumball-Gally	Henry Duffield	340	30	56	Borneo & China	August 6.
O	Sidney	Lewis Whitwell	475	36	95	Bengall	9.
E	Neptune	George Lafhly	270	22	55	China	September 21.
E	Northumberland	Charles Richards	250	24	50	Ditto	22.
E	Exton-Frigate	George Philips	340	27	68	Ditto	Ditto
E	Dafhwood	Marmaduke Royden	320	26	64	Ditto	Ditto
E	Seaford	Martin Gardner	240	24	46	Ditto	Ditto
E	Stretham	Roger Myers	350	30	70	Coaft & Bay	Ditto
E	Jofiah	Randolph Pye	500	36	100	Bay of Bengall	Ditto
O P	Goffright	Edward Harrifon	330	30	50	China	Ditto
+ E	Summers-Frigate	Jofeph North	460	32	97	Bay of Bengall	24.

The Anne, Adam Spencer, was blown up May the 4th, near the Isle of Wight, returning Home.

LONDON. Printed for and Sold by *Edward Lloyd*, at his Coffee Houfe in *Lombard Street*. October the 5th. 1702.

(Corporation of Lloyd's collection)

A Ships' List published by Edward Lloyd in 1702

CHAPTER 1   LLOYD'S COFFEE HOUSE

IT is an odd circumstance that the two most venerable organisations
concerned in the prime British industry of shipping take their
names from the same somewhat shadowy person—Edward Lloyd,
who kept a coffee house in the City of London during the Restoration
period.

These institutions are Lloyd's, the great Insurance Corporation,
and Lloyd's Register of Shipping, wholly engaged in the classification
of ships and the maintenance of technical standards in shipbuilding,
and, latterly, public works, oilfield installations and so on. In
spite of popular confusions, however, they are quite separate
bodies, each with its separate history. This book is wholly concerned
with that of Lloyd's Register of Shipping during the two centuries of
its existence; and it is perhaps worth noting at this early stage,

B

if only to make confusion less confounded, that Lloyds Bank did not spring from the same roots and has no place in this narrative.

As to the common progenitor of Lloyd's and Lloyd's Register of Shipping very little of a personal kind is known. Even the Dictionary of National Biography cannot give him a date of birth and is content to suggest that he flourished between 1688 and 1726. (Other records suggest that he died in 1713.) How he looked and spoke we know not. Edward Lloyd was a Welshman; for the rest he remains a legend, the founder of a convivial institution that in due course gave birth to two institutions of the largest commercial importance.

This man first opened a coffee house in Tower Street, London, attracting to his place of business many of those who made their livings out of the shipping that used London River. The maritime strength of Britain was then increasing rapidly, and the most influential men in this expanding department of commerce were tending to set up their counting houses in the City proper, near the Royal Exchange and the Bank of England. Lloyd therefore transferred himself and his catering enterprise to Lombard Street, at the corner of Abchurch Lane.

This was the true birthplace of the institutions that still carry his name to immortality in their titles. Here Edward Lloyd created a sort of club, to which every man of consequence in the shipping business found it prudent to belong. The histories and influences of those London coffee houses of the day before yesterday are in themselves fruitful subjects of study, but it is enough for the moment that Lloyd's was one of the most outstanding in its own period and, considering what grew out of it, is now certainly the most famous.

That it was recognised as important in its own period is implicit in the fact that Steele in the *Tatler* and Addison in the *Spectator* both wrote about it. Unfortunately, neither of these essays is among its author's best. Both are "topical" in the sense that the reader's knowledge of the subject is taken for granted; neither gives what the modern reader would fain have—a visual description of the place and some suggestion of its atmosphere. Steele's essay is the more rewarding in that respect. Apparently he visited Lloyd's on an invitation accompanied by the gift of "a parcel of port", and we may surmise that the shrewd Welshman in Edward Lloyd was looking for the favour of a great journalist of the period.

2

The general picture is of a rather crowded and noisy club, in which the members spent most of the day over cups containing beverages more exciting than coffee. Much of the time was filled with auctions; and from other sources we gather that these were of strangely varied lots—parcels of wine, shares in ships, the cargoes of prizes of war, and even leasehold estates. Steele's attention was mainly attracted by a sort of pulpit from which, despite the din about him, one of Lloyd's servants read loudly and continuously. The important announcements were items of shipping intelligence, but when these were in short supply the reader, or announcer, would entertain the company with a contemporary ballad or topical skit. A pulpit is to this day a feature of Lloyd's in its capacity as a marine insurance corporation, and from this rostrum its more important announcements are delivered.

Both Steele and Addison fail us by neglecting the importance of Lloyd's coffee house as an exchange of shipping news and the nature of the limited but peculiar genius of Edward Lloyd himself. That canny innkeeper devoted serious thought to the art of attracting and keeping custom, and he was prolific in devices to establish his house as the chosen rendezvous of the most influential men in the shipping business. Whatever he may have done before in the way of circulating information on handwritten sheets, in 1696 he began to print and issue thrice weekly the bulletin of shipping and commercial information to which he gave the name of *Lloyd's News*. This lasted only a few months, an indiscreet reference to proceedings in the House of Lords bringing upon his head the disapproval of the Government.

In its place, Lloyd printed and circulated among his patrons bulletins, or Ships' Lists, giving brief descriptions of ships likely to be offered for insurance, but in the absence of any organised system of survey the details were perhaps few and sketchy. One of these bulletins, dated 5th October, 1702, is reproduced at the beginning of this chapter. The newspaper was revived in 1734, however, as *Lloyd's List* and has appeared regularly ever since—with the exception of the official *London Gazette* the oldest newspaper now in existence.

The outlines of history are blurred hereabouts by the intrusion of legend. It has frequently been asserted that an organised *Register of Shipping* appeared in 1760. If so, no copy has survived. On the other hand, the title page of one of the earliest of the authentic Register

Books clearly states that it was the creation of a committee formed in that year—that is, out of underwriters and brokers within the orbit of Lloyd's. This seems to explain a popular confusion. Indeed, it may fairly be held to suggest that the earliest extant volume of the Register Book, that for 1764–65–66, was the first fruit of the labours of the committee appointed in 1760. There is no doubt that Lloyd's Register of Shipping is in proper historical order in celebrating its bi-centenary in 1960.

The business of insuring vessels and their cargoes on their lawful occasions started just as soon as men of one nation began trading with those of another in the mighty waters. The Phœnicians, the Venetians, the Hanseatic merchants—all had their systems of insurance against the hazards of the sea; and some of the Italian Republics regulated the depth beyond which a vessel should not be loaded, the equivalent of what is popularly known nowadays as the Plimsoll Line. There is the detached word of Edward Gibbon for it that in A.D. 533 the Justinian Laws of Rome, dealing with legal rates of usury, specially provided for the exemption of rates of marine insurance, "a perilous adventure".

On the face of it, the underwriter called upon to accept a maritime risk and the shippers of a valuable cargo would seek some guarantee of the fitness of the vessel concerned for the voyage in prospect. It was inevitable that the underwriters, now cohering as a group within the cheerful premises of Mr. Lloyd, should set up some system of inspection of hulls and equipment. Probably the "Ships' Lists" circulating in Lloyd's Coffee House were written by hand in the first place; possibly the ingenious Lloyd started to have them printed when he took to publishing his own newspaper. They were still without authority, even if they had the value of stimulating the underwriters towards the ideal of scientific classification. That was the common origin of the Corporation of Lloyd's and of Lloyd's Register of Shipping. Many years were to pass before the Corporation of Lloyd's and Lloyd's Register of Shipping were to become separate concerns, but when the man-in-the-street uses the locution "A1 at Lloyd's", without quite fully realising the fact he means that the Corporation of Lloyd's, as underwriters, are guaranteed a first-class risk as defined by the surveyors, Lloyd's Register of Shipping.

At length, in 1769, the leading underwriters and brokers deserted

Former	Present	Master	Port	To Port	Ton²	Guns	M Built & Year	Owners	64	65	66
D	Daking —	Wm. Taylor	Lond.	Cork	150	S D B b	12 Liverp. 60	Daking & Co	E M	E M	
	Dalrymple —	Jun⁵ Berry	Liverp.	Old Cl. & Am.	120 s	B	Welch 57	Davenport	E M	E M	
	Dankbarhey⁶	Cos Mandertz	Lond.	Amsterdam	160	S d	8 Amſterd. 62	Feitama	A G	A G	
	Dant. Packet —	Hoiſley		Riga	200		11 River 54	Belford	E M	E M	
Gen. Pacᵗ	Darby —	Hᶠ Boardman		Dublin	80	S D	7 Plantation 61	J. Boardman			
	Darlington	MᶜLauglin		Quebec	200	D B	12 River 56	P. Weathrall	E M	E M	
	David & Eliz.	John Brown		Rotterdam	90 s	S L	8 Colcheſter 62	David Baker	A G	A G	
	Dawes —	John Forbes		Jamaica	300 s	6	3 Ipſwich 63	H. Mure	A G		
	Dawkins —	R. Balentine		Mad. & Jam.	250 s	4	20 River 49	Alex. Grant	E M		
	Dean —	Jno Saliſbury		Dublin	130		12 Cheſter 50	John Dean			
Neptune	Dear Beſsey	B. Beale	Liverp.	Cork & Barb'	90 s	B	8 Plantation 56	Doran & Co.	E M		
	Deep Bay	Wm. Oliver	Lond.	St. Kitt's	180		13	J. & J. Mills	A G		
	Deep Bay —	S. Daſhwood		Boſton	150	B	10 Boſton 63	Lane & Booth	A G		
	Defiance —	Shutter	Liverp.	Larne	50	B	6 Britiſh 60		E M		
Jupiter	Degartiquert	Rettine	Lond.	Hamburgh	100		5 Amſterd. 61	Rettine			
	Delaware —	. Jolly		Nap. & Meſ.	300 s 16	2	3 Plantation 62	J. Jolly	E M		
	Delaware —	Pet. Creaton			150		10 Philadel. 61	Wharton	A G		
	Delight —	W. Richardᶠ	Liverp.	Bon. & Am.	120 s		20 French 56	Rumbold & C	E M		
Matthew	Delight —	R. Birtam	Yarm.	Naples	130	S d B	8 Yarmouth 53	Wm. Fiſher	A G		
	Denia Caſtle	ohn Irwin	Lond.	Streights	100	B	9 Plantation 60	C. Conner	A M		
	Devonſhire	H. Hunter		Boſton	160		10 Boſton 61	John Roe	A M		
Reaves —	Devonſhire	Rich. Aſhton		Pᵗ Gᵉ Bˢ & Wᵉ	200 s 8	4	15 French 58	Lewis Teſier	E M		
	DeVrow Joa²	Pet. Smidt		Amſterdam	200		12 Amſterd. 53	Tiddiman	E M		
Genˡ Frᵈ	Diadem —	Evan Johnſon		Leghorn	364 s 8	6	20 French 50	Twitoe & C.	E M		
	Diamond —	Wm. Stott		Gen. & Leg.	280 16	4	3 Rive 41	Franco	E G		

A page of the 1764-5-6 Register

the hospitable rooms of Edward Lloyd's successors and set up a place of their own in Pope's Head Alley, Cornhill, calling it the New Lloyd's Coffee House. After a few years there they removed themselves and their documents to the Royal Exchange. And the Royal Exchange was destroyed by fire in 1838.

This conflagration is part of the legend of the City of London. It happened on a February night so bitterly cold that, we are told, the water froze as it emerged from the hoses. It is solemnly recorded that, as the building collapsed, the chimes in the tower were playing the melody of "There's Nae Luck aboot the Hoose"—a romantic touch and at least *ben trovato*. The flames did in fact consume most of the documents belonging to Lloyd's as a separate body, and, of course, most of those pertaining to the special branch of survey and registration. There did survive, however, slightly charred, a copy of the "Register of Shipping" for the years 1764-65-66. This is the Holy Bible of Lloyd's Register of Shipping and as such is reverently preserved in the library of the present Headquarters at 71, Fenchurch Street, London, E.C.3.

It is a smallish volume, oblong in shape. A specimen page reproduced herewith shows that the printing was of very decent quality. This was done by W. Richardson and S. Clark, in Fleet Street, almost certainly the successors of Samuel Richardson, that "stout, rosy, vain, prosy little man" who was one of the fathers of the English novel. It is seen that the details of the ships listed were remarkably full; and this in its turn suggests that the new Register had in fact been in preparation for some years before this survivor of the fire was published.

Most of the entries are obvious, if the spelling of place names is apt to be eccentric. One notes that most of the vessels were armed in the age of free-for-all warfare at sea. The ships in the list are given such antique notations as SdB, signifying single deck with tier of supporting beams, and so on. The columns headed 65 and 66 provide space for symbols to be assigned as the result of later surveys, but that headed 64 is the one of greatest interest to us to-day. This gives in symbolic capital letters the classification conferred on the ship by the Committee's appointed surveyors.

The hulls of ships were classified A, E, I, O, or U, according to the excellence of their construction and their continuing soundness, or otherwise. Equipment was G, M or B—simply good, middling or bad. Any vessel classified AG was thus as sound as it could be, while one rated UB was obviously a bad risk from the underwriter's point of view. As we have noted, the extra columns headed 65 and 66 provide for notes on the improvement or deterioration of the ship's fabric, usually the latter.

The second Register, of which a copy is extant in the library of the office in Fenchurch Street, is dated 1768–69. This book differs considerably from the first in respect of both make-up and classification. It catalogues the rig of ships listed, for example, reports on repairs effected, and leaves columns blank for the "posting" by hand of other changes made during subsequent years.

The most considerable change, however, is an alteration of the symbols of classification. The old capital letters A, E, I, O and U, are dropped and replaced by small letters printed above the line, thus ^{a}, ^{b} and ^{c}; the condition of equipment is described by the numerals 1, 2, 3 and 4. Thus a ship previously classed AG is now designated ^{a}1, and so on.

The third oldest Register preserved in the library is dated 1775–76, and a page is reproduced herewith. In general arrangement the book closely resembles its predecessor, but in this case the authorities reverted to Roman capitals for the classification of the hull and used only the numerals 1 and 2 for the description of the equipment. Thus a vessel in the highest category was classed A1, and that was almost certainly the origin of the legendary phrase. This third book is also a landmark in that alterations are posted weekly in type instead of with pen and ink: a practice that has been a feature of Lloyd's Register Book ever since.

These three earliest books lack the front covers and the opening pages, but they are obviously workmanlike jobs. The third sets a standard of presentation that, with a few minor variations, was maintained for some years thereafter: for example, the introduction of lists of ships of the Royal Navy and the East India Company. The file of Registers from 1775 onwards is complete. In the earlier years of its existence it was known, for reasons that will appear later on, as the Underwriters' Register or, even more popularly, as the Green Book. As for the alterations of symbols during the first ten years of its existence, these were almost certainly due to changes of organisation

	Ship		Master	Tons	Built		Owner		Destined		
2	Cadiz Packet	Wm Collins / Wm Pearl	200	River	67	M.Campion	13	Lo. Cadiz / Lo.Transpt	A.1	A.1
		S s 73								8	
3	—	S	A.Crnelius	300	Whitby	73	Capt. & Co.		Wy.Oftnd	A.1	3
4	—	Sp	E. Thomas	70	Wales	71	M Hmphrys	8	CoDublin	A.2	73
	Sea-flower	SD									6
5	Cæcilia Bg		Js Neal	100	N.Engld	62	R Arthur&C	11	StUbesCo	E.2	
					trp. 73						
6	Cæfar	S s	Ja Curry	200	Marylnd	68	Jn Campbell	13	Lo. Jamai. C.	E.1	E.1
	Two Friends 69				grp.70, lrp. 73					5	6
7	—	Sk	Jn Doyle	50	Irifh	61	J Perkins&C	8	Li.NFifh	E.1	
					lrp. 75					6	
8	—	Sw s	W Grayfon	160	Whithvn	50	Capt.	13	Wn Cork	E.2	I.2
		SDB			feveral rep.					3	2
9	—	Sw s	E. Larveo	130	Sthmptn	47	T. Hindley		StraitsLo.	E.1	E.2
										73	8
10	—	S	Wm Miller	250	Philadel.	74	Neave & Co.	17	Jamai.Lo.	A.1	A.1
	Now the Jul.Cefar, Wzield									5	5
1	—	S s	L. O'Brian	200	Bofton A.	67	Lane & Co.	13	LoGrnads C.	E.1	E.1
					N.U.W. 73					5	10
2	—	S s	Jn Sullivan	180	America	63	Capt.	15	Milfrd Co	E.1	
	Alexander				trp.71					73	
3	—	Sw	Wm Wood	180	Briftol	73	Lepincot &c	13	Br. Virgin / Br.Grnads	A.1	A.1
		s 76								2	3
4	—	S s	W Wethral / C.Merriton	250	Virginia	73	Capt. & Co.	14	Virgin Lo. / Lo. Tranfpr	A.1	A.1
		73		192						1	
5	Calais Packet	Jof. Rofs / Jn Stanbak	60	Fevrfhm	64	Wm Gilby	8	Lo. Calais C.	E.1	E.1
	Sp	SD								1	7
6	Calcutta		W Thmpfn	761	River	70			Bombay / 2d Voyage	—	74
7	Calvert	S s 76	Wm Sewell	350	Marylnd	72	M. Molleson	16	Lo. Mryld	A.1	A.1
		SDB								10	
8	Camberwell	S s	Jn Forbes / P.Ogilvie	150	Shorham	64	Al. Brander	13	Lo.Lifbon C.	E.2	E.1
										2	4
9	Cambletown	Bg d 58	D. Stewart	305	River	45	Walker &C.	14	Lh Grnld C.	I.2	I.2
					trp.73					2	
20	Cambridge	Sw s 74	Rt Hutton	140	N.Engld	64	Wm Horner	11	Li Virgin. / Li.Baltic	I.1	I.1
		SDB			D.rp. 74					3	
1	Camden	S s 74	J. Richrdfn	300	Hamptn	65	S. Grove	14	Lo. Mryld / Lo.Autigua	A.1	A.1
		SDB								5	
2	—	S s	H. Wright	300	Marylnd	75	Everard &C	13	Ly Norwy	A.1	A.1
		SDB								10	2
3	Camelia Bg s	Rt Aynfley	60	River	48	Capt.	8	Lo. Africa	E.1	
	Joseph & Mary	SD								9	
4	Campbell Sw s	J Suthrland	180	Briftol	74	D.Hamilton	16	Br Grnads C.	A.1	A.1
		75				6 --- 4 P.				10	6
25	Canadian S s	Wm Abbot	200	N.Engld	72	B Watfn&C.	14	LoHallifx	A.1	A.1
		74								9	7

A page of the 1775–6 Register. In this book the
classification symbol A1 was used for the first time

within Lloyd's as it developed out of and away from the coffee house stage.

It is important to understand that these early Registers were produced under the auspices of Lloyd's as a society of underwriters and brokers, however loosely constituted at that period. The day on which the Register was to be completely separated from Lloyd's as underwriters was still far distant. In fact, the underwriters—now calling themselves "Members of the Society"—cherished their Green Book with a sort of animal jealousy and made stringent regulations to the end of keeping its contents virtually secret.

Each subscriber must deliver up his old copy before a new one could be issued to him. If a book were lost or stolen, the owner was refused another, even if willing to pay for it. A set of by-laws printed in the volume for 1779–80 starts quaintly:—

> "As the interest of the Society is, in the first Instance, greatly hurt by the Custom of shewing the Books, and leaving them at Places where they are but too common, thereby preventing many Underwriters from becoming Members, who, though they reap the Advantages and Benefits in common with them, do not pay their Quota towards the expenses of the Institution, thereby, as much as in them lies, reducing the Members to the Necessity of paying larger Subscriptions . . ."

and goes on to set out a scale of fines and forfeits for the sin of showing the Book to unqualified persons and for its loss.

This exclusiveness did not notably increase the popularity of the underwriters of Lloyd's among the shipowners and shipbuilders outside their own London circle. The appearance of the Register for 1797–98 brought to a head a storm that had been gathering over a period of years.

This volume introduced still another style of classification. The new symbols were to be M for the first class of vessel, G for the second, L for the third, and Z for the distinctly inferior. The numerals 8 and 4 were to designate the quality of equipment. The most staggering of the new rules, however, laid it down that a ship built on the Thames could remain in the first class for a term of thirteen years, while another of the same description built at an outport would remain in the top class for eight years only. Preference was even given to ships built in Canada. Owners outside London were further exasperated by the refusal of classification to ships taken as prizes, then being brought into the western estuaries in considerable numbers.

It was on the face of it unreasonable to maintain that a ship built on the Thames—or on the St. Lawrence—was *ipso facto* a better job than one built on the Wear or on Belfast Lough; and the distinction was impolitic, to say the least of it. But if it seems to us now a curious case of provincialism in reverse, it was really not so unreasonable as it appears to us to-day.

London was then, as now, the greatest port in the United Kingdom. Its shipowners controlled the vast bulk of foreign trade and knew more than anybody else about the general character of the mercantile marine of that period. As a witness from Hull was to put it at an Inquiry later on, "ships built on the River Thames are unquestionably better than those built at outports; the London builders obtain better prices, and can therefore afford to build them of a better description". More than that, the northern rivers were still far from making to the total output of new British tonnage the large contribution they make to-day. Indeed, the Clyde, later to become the largest centre of production by dint of its early specialisation in steam propulsion and iron hulls, was negligible in the terms of 1790.

However that may be, the discriminations suggested by the Register of 1797–98 provoked shipping interests outside London to action. The opposition was nominally led by a "Society of Merchants, Ship-owners and Underwriters," but it appears that the shipowners dominated the movement; and though resentment of the new Lloyd's scheme of classification was particularly strong in Sunderland, then one of the busiest shipbuilding centres beyond the Thames, this new Society had its offices in London: first at No. 22, Change Alley, and afterwards at No. 3, St. Michael's Alley. Its Committee consisted of 15 members, with a Mr. John Hill as chairman. It is apparent that though the revolt was warmly supported by interests outside London, the movement had its main strength within the City itself—as it were a palace revolution aimed at the hegemony Lloyd's had assumed.

These dissatisfied persons first made urgent representations of protest to Lloyd's and were rebuffed. The shipowners then formed their own committee, started to raise subscriptions, and proceeded to make arrangements, necessarily complicated, for the publication of a Register Book of their own. The sheer difficulty of setting up new organisations for survey, registration and certification is a measure of the gravity of the war now about to break out.

This it did in 1799 with the appearance of *The New Register Book of Shipping*. This became known familiarly as the Shipowners' Register, or Red Book, as distinct from the Underwriters' Register, the Green Book. Its appearance started a battle that was to last for nearly 35 years and to prove nearly ruinous to both parties. We can see it now, however, as a first step in the process whereby Lloyd's Register of Shipping was ultimately separated completely from Lloyd's as an underwriting group.

The importance of the Register within Lloyd's had already been recognised by the appointment of a Committee to supervise that special branch of the general underwriting business. It is obvious, surely, that even the first lists circulated within Edward Lloyd's coffee house must have been organised; still more so that the first Registers were compiled with authority. It was not until the Book of 1797–98 appeared, however, that the existence of a guiding body was openly revealed.

This was a committee presided over by Mr. John Julius Angerstein, with 11 members in all. Mr. Angerstein was also Chairman of Lloyd's proper, and this fact alone speaks for the great importance attached to the business of classification. Indeed, history must look on John Julius Angerstein as the first known Chairman of what was to become Lloyd's Register of Shipping. As for this special committee, there is nothing now to show how it was elected, but it is a fair assumption that it existed with a certain degree of independence, that it kept up its numbers by the simple device of co-option, and that it changed the system of classification without consulting the Subscribers at large. (One may fairly wonder if the revolt of the shipowners was not against the exclusiveness of this cabal within the circle of underwriters.) At all events the Underwriters' Register occupied offices of its own at an early stage: first in Sun Court and subsequently in Castle Court, Birchin Lane.

Let us remember again that the subscribers to the early books described themselves as "Members of the Society" without any special reference to membership of Lloyd's. The volume for 1777–78, definitely sponsored by Lloyd's, lists 130 of them, including the two great marine insurance companies of the day, the Royal Exchange and the London Assurance—both large subscribers towards the costs of production.

The constitution of Lloyd's Register of Shipping is to this day slightly ambiguous from the strict legal point of view, but it is at least clear that, during the first 30-odd years of existence in its first form, it had acquired a degree of cohesion and independence as well as certain powers of its own. The latter were to be needed during the first three decades of the 19th Century, for the shipowners with their Red Book were formidable rivals, and with a good deal of justice on their side.

CHAPTER 2   GREEN AND RED

IF the appearance of the Red Book opened a long war with a
resounding salvo, the Shipowners prefaced the new publication
with a reasonable and quite elegantly phrased statement of their aims.
They started by acknowledging the great value of the Green Book in
its earlier editions and the soundness of the original system of classification; but then

> "In the preceding year 1798, the Committee of the Society, with-
> out consulting the Subscribers at large, made an entire change in
> this system, so long established and universally approved, and sub-
> stituted in its place a plan founded on a principle diametrically
> opposite and perfectly erroneous."

The preface goes on to examine in detail, and with appropriate

11

scorn, the fallacies in the system of classifying ships according to the place of building, and proceeds loftily

> "No general reasons have been assigned for the new plan; and, as to the distinction of places, imagination is left to its free scope to ascertain what causes make some situations so inferior to others; for instance, why should ships built at Quebec stand in the first class two years longer than vessels built at Hull or the Northern ports of this kingdom, Wales, etc? and professional men are equally at a loss to conjecture why the Committee have thought proper to class the shipping of some ports in these kingdoms in degrees so much inferior to that of others . . ."

A final passage quotes one of the resolutions reached at a protest meeting to the grave effect that the Underwriters' system would "in a great measure tend to destroy the shipping of the country."

The system of classification put forward in the Red Book, while inevitably rejecting that based on the place of building, was a return to the earlier manner of the Green Book. It provided for four classes—A, E, I and O—and for two grades of "ship's materials" or equipment, expressed in the numerals 1 and 2. It still maintained a slight preference in favour of the Thames-built vessel, if entirely of British oak and well fastened, giving it 12 years in class A1 as against ten years for the "country-built" ship. Class E included older ships without defects revealed by survey and capable of carrying safely a dry cargo—that is, a cargo liable to damage by contact with sea water. The third class, marked I, was made up of vessels which, though not in tip-top shape, were deemed sufficiently seaworthy to carry cargoes other than those described as dry. In class O were the despised and rejected, judged unfit for foreign voyaging.

These changes went far to mollify those who had protested against the Underwriters' discrimination in favour of the Thames-built ship, but the Shipowners' regulations perpetuated two sources of irritation. One was that any vessel automatically lapsed to an inferior grade on the expiry of the original classification; no matter how much time and money and care might be lavished on her repair and overhaul, she could never again be classed A1. Nor was provision made for such stringent Rules as nowadays govern the construction of any ship, or for systematic survey. Finally, there was next to no supervision of surveyors, so that the standards must have varied widely from port to port.

Both systems embodied these grave defects, and it was not very long before a large body of opinion in all branches of the shipping industry were crying a plague on both their houses. It seems strange to us to-day that, in matters of such vital importance to Britain and its increasing wealth in colonial possessions, the rivalry was allowed to go on and on without the intervention of the government. But so it was; and a history of the proceedings could be made to read like a comic account of the bickerings of two groups of ill-tempered old gentlemen.

The opening of the battle is nicely dated from the turn of the century, 1800. At the beginning of that year the Green Book could boast 233 subscribers, the Red Book only 125. In the course of the year 1800, however, the latter acquired 76 new subscribers, the former only 31. This seems to have shaken the Underwriters to the extent that, in their next issue of the Green Book, they reverted to the original symbols of classification, A, E, I, O and U. Among minor alterations they boasted on a title page that the work had been "Instituted in 1760"—an obvious pass at the upstart opposition. To this the Shipowners retorted in the preface to the third edition of their Red Book that, while the Underwriters might seem to have had second thoughts, "it will be found, on inspection, that the new plan is still adhered to, namely, that of giving characters to ships according to their ages and the places where built, without a due regard to the manner in which they were originally built, the repairs they have received, and their actual state and condition".

Under this sort of attack the Underwriters yielded another inch or two of ground, allowing in editions of the Green Book published in the early years of the century classifications to prize vessels and ships of dubious age that had previously been treated as less than the dust. Soon the parties were engaged, however, in what we have learned to call economic warfare.

Early copies of the Red Book now in the library of Lloyd's Register in Fenchurch Street indicate that its subscribers paid for it at the rate of eight guineas a year. This was almost certainly responsible for the decision of the Underwriters in 1810 to reduce the subscription for the Green Book to the same figure—that is, down to eight guineas from twelve. So it went on, very little more dignified than a circulation war between newspaper groups in Fleet Street to-day.

As to the relative values of the two Registers for ordinary reference purposes, the Green Book listed 8,271 vessels in its edition of 1800, while the second edition of the Red Book in the same year carried particulars of 7,754 vessels. A year later the Red Book raced ahead, carrying particulars of 9,540 ships against 9,145 in the Green Book. But these figures, like the rivalry itself, were sadly divorced from reality. To neither Society did a shipowner pay a fee when submitting his ship for survey, so that many vessels were listed in both books. The prosperity of either could be measured only by the number of paying subscribers, and these dwindled as the years passed, more and more of the neutrals within the shipping industry holding back in despair of, if not disgust with, the antics of Underwriters and Ship-owners in their war of attrition.

Both parties had so exhausted themselves by 1833 that it looked as if both Registers must shut up shop within a year or so. The Green Book had now only 163 subscribers, and its funds were down to little more than £1,000. The Red Book was supported by only 75 sub-scribers, and the shipowners who supported it were dipping into their private pockets to keep it going. There was thus the alarming prospect of an island nation, its maritime trade rapidly increasing, being left without any system of classification or any sort of Register at all.

This grim prospect had been envisaged ten years before. In 1823 the General Shipowners' Society, led by an enlightened man from Hull, Mr. John Marshall, had sought to start a movement towards amalgamation. This Society convened a meeting of interested parties at the London Tavern, Bishopsgate, on December 11th that year, a Mr. George Lyall in the chair. From Marshall's notes of the proceed-ings at this and subsequent gatherings we gather that both Registers had already fallen into disrepute, and that both were heading slowly but surely towards financial ruin. In one of his speeches this John Marshall said—referring to the situation in 1823–24:—

> "The Old Book has about 180 Subscribers, at eight guineas each, and twenty guineas each from the Royal Exchange and London Assurance Companies, which gives, as I assume, an income of £1,550; the New Book has about 126 Subscribers, at the same rate, and with two similar donations, realises about £1,080. If, instead of two, only one Book was published, and that on a principle which would combine general approbation, the aggregate number of Sub-

14

scribers would, I conceive, be much increased, and the ability to pay fit and competent Surveyors and other necessary and efficient officers of the establishment, proportionably augmented. The number of vessels registered in the Old Book is, in round numbers, about 14,450; in the New one, about 13,950; and upon so numerous a Marine, a revenue might, in my opinion, be raised, without any undue pressure on its Proprietors, fully adequate to the expenses of an establishment in all respects efficient for its object."

In other speeches Marshall inveighed against the Underwriters' Committee in particular as being composed of men representing only one branch of the shipping industry, "self-elected and wholly irresponsible". He objected strongly, and with justice, to the decisions of the surveyors being uncontrolled and final. His best point was that the system of classification wholly by age and origin really created a glut of tonnage, for since a vessel that had outlived her first classification could not be restored to her first rating by any amount of repair and overhaul, the owner was forced to discard and replace her with a new ship in order to acquire "the talismanic charm of A1".

These and other arguments were accepted unanimously at the meeting already mentioned, and a motion that a committee of inquiry, representative of shipowners, merchants and underwriters, be set up to examine the position was enthusiastically confirmed by a large gathering held on January 22nd, 1824, Mr. Thomas Wilson, M.P., in the chair.

This was a promising move, but it was soon to be checked by conservatism, and it must be admitted that some subscribers from within Lloyd's were the dogs in the manger. They met on February 18th, 1824, and the Chairman of the Committee of Lloyd's, Mr. Benjamin Shaw, opened with a fighting speech, in which he declared that, while the existing system of classification might not be free from objection, it suited the underwriters very well. Thus, "the proposal that Lloyd's should concur in the suggested investigation, by appointing eight of their members to form part of a committee of inquiry, was a measure which they strongly deprecated". Mr. John Marshall again protested, declaring almost tearfully, "All that is now asked for is inquiry . . ."; and his subsequent plea, couched in the choicest periods of early 19th century oratory, so moved the meeting that a resolution to take part in the inquiry was passed with only two dissentients.

The result so far was therefore the creation of a split within the membership of Lloyd's—a piquant and significant indication of the way the wind was blowing. Another General Meeting of the Members of Lloyd's was called for March 3rd, 1824. The familiar ground was gone all over again, and a good deal of heat was engendered. In the issue, the opponents of inquiry demanded a ballot.

A short and sharp campaign ensued. The Committee of Lloyd's circulated their report against inquiry, and Mr. Marshall retorted with a manifesto for the other side. The voting took place between one and four o'clock on Wednesday, March 10th, 1824. The rest can be left to the ecstatic pen of Marshall himself:—

> "The intense interest created by it, the feelings exhibited in its progress, and the extraordinary efforts made by most of those who so mistakenly exerted their opposition, will never be forgotten by the *friends of inquiry*, who on that day supported the moderate and reasonable proposition submitted to them. Suffice it to say, Reason triumphed! No less than *six hundred and seventy-nine Members of Lloyd's* voted on that occasion: almost every counting-house and coffee-house in the City being visited to procure the attendance of every Subscriber who could be found; the result, however, was that the Resolution 'That Lloyd's do concur in nominating eight of their Body to represent them in the Committee of Inquiry', was confirmed on the ballot by a majority of twenty-five—there being 352 *for* and 327 *against it*!"

In this way, late in the day and while the rivalry of the Green and Red Books was exhausting their respective promoters, the Committee of Inquiry was set up. It consisted of 33 members, those from London in a large majority. Out of the City came 24 members, eight each from among the Merchants, the Shipowners and the Underwriters respectively. Nine men represented the outports—Liverpool, Hull, Glasgow, Newcastle, Whitby, Sunderland, Yarmouth, Leith and Whitehaven & Maryport. This was apparently the first recognition of Glasgow as a leading outport, perhaps a reflection of the growing importance of vessels powered by steam. The vigorous Mr. John Marshall was included as the representative of Hull. The appointed Chairman was Mr. James Lindsay, Junr., of Lloyd's.

The proceedings of these 33 good men and true were conducted with vigour. They took evidence and opinions from the Commissioners and Surveyors of H.M. Navy, from the Master-Builder of the

Royal Dockyard at Deptford, from the Principal Surveyor to the Hon. East India Company, from the Surveyors of the existing Registry Books, and from the Shipowners' Societies in the leading outports. A whole army of individuals contributed specialised knowledge and impartial opinion. In the end, the Committee boasted that "the evidence must stand far beyond the reach of impeachment or suspicion".

It took nearly two years to reach its conclusions, but the Report at length made available on February 8th, 1826, appears to have been unanimous. Its observations were forceful. The international importance of the Books was stressed; it was necessary for the credit of Britain as a seafaring nation that it should set up one standard of classification, and that of the highest quality. The principles of the existing system of classification were "most fallacious and erroneous", while "the partial degree of actual survey required by the system" was "rendered practically nugatory by the insufficiency of the salaries paid to the Surveyors". It finally proposed the formation of a completely new Society with a new set of Rules. The proposed constitution was as follows:—

> "That the future Superintendence of the Classification of Shipping be entrusted to a Committee in London, to be composed of thirty-two Members, consisting of six Merchants and six Shipowners of London, to be appointed by a General Meeting of Merchants and Shipowners, respectively; six Members of Lloyd's, to be appointed by that body; one Representative by the Royal Exchange, London, Alliance, and Mutual Indemnity Assurance Associations, respectively; and one Representative resident in London for each of the following Outports, viz.: Liverpool, Hull, Glasgow, Newcastle, Bristol, Whitby, Yarmouth, Leith, Whitehaven, and Sunderland.
>
> "That two Members of those appointed by the Shipowners, two of those deputed by the Merchants of London, and two of the Members of Lloyd's, should go out of office annually, but be eligible for re-election; and the appointment of the Outport Representatives be during the pleasure of their Constituents.
>
> "Such Committee to appoint a Chairman and Deputy-Chairman, Secretary, and Assistants, and all the Surveyors both for London and the Outports; and to be restricted in their proceedings to a conformity with the Rules and Regulations under which they may be appointed; but to have full power to make such Bye-Laws for their own government and proceedings as they may deem requisite, not being inconsistent with their original constitution."

C

The classifications suggested are not of importance at the moment, but the Committee of Inquiry hammered most valuably at the importance of having a large, qualified staff of competent and independent surveyors. It suggested that these qualified officers should be stationed throughout the country, subject to the supervision of Principal Surveyors appointed in London and able to travel to the outports as required. The duties of all surveyors were set out in precise detail. Most important—in the light of future events—provision was to be made for the stringent inspection of vessels *while under construction*. In many ways the Report adumbrated many of the leading general principles according to which Lloyd's Register of Shipping operates to-day.

Nor did the Committee of Inquiry fail thoroughly to examine the financial prospects of the new Register their report envisaged. It was estimated that its establishment and maintenance would cost about £13,700 per annum. This allowed £7,700 for the salaries of 34 surveyors, at rates ranging from £600 downwards to £150, but only £75 in the cases of a few minor ports. The sum of £6,000 was earmarked for what we would nowadays call administration. Taking into account the changed value of money, the scale of salaries proposed for the surveyors was handsome; this Committee never once lost sight of the fact that a sound Register could be guaranteed only by the appointment of skilled men who, carefully selected, could work with complete detachment.

But—a nearly fatal "but" in this case—the Committee also concluded reluctantly that the sort of Register they proposed could hardly be established and maintained on a voluntary basis. They thought that, without subsidy from the Government, the prospect of raising sufficient monies "must, except under the sanction and authority of Parliamentary provision, prove visionary and hopeless". They admitted that "direct interposition of public support would, in all probability, transfer to the Executive Government the superintendence of a system imperatively requiring for its effective administration the aid of mercantile and professional knowledge and experience". Reasoned objection to the principle of Nationalisation is thus no novelty!

The hesitation of the Committee of Inquiry in this single respect of finance had undoubtedly the effect of subduing enthusiasm for the Report in its practical aspects. The document was put before a general meeting of all parties concerned on June 1st, 1826, Thomas Wilson, M.P., in the chair. The supreme moment at this gathering was the reading of a letter from the Board of Trade. This intimated that "the Board approved highly of the proposed alterations, and were of opinion that it would give rise to great improvements in the naval architecture of the country; and that the Lords of their Committee would be disposed to assist in carrying the proposed regulations into effect, in any manner which might, on subsequent discussion, be deemed advisable". In other words, our blessing but no subsidy.

It seems to us, who nowadays take the position of Lloyd's Register of Shipping for granted as that of supreme authority in several fields of technical excellence besides that of shipping: as an institution of almost sacred probity in international opinion . . . it seems very strange indeed that the findings of the Committee of Inquiry were to be thrown aside. But so it turned out.

The failure cannot be wholly attributed to Whitehall's evasion of any promise to help financially towards the launching of the new scheme. As in all affairs of moment in which conflicting human elements are engaged there was no single cause of the curious delays that followed the gallant meeting on June 1st, 1826. For one thing, some of the older and more eager protagonists of reform passed away in the course of nature. For another, there lingered among the underwriters much of the old diehard spirit. Worst of all, however, was that slowest and subtlest of all enemies of progress—the sheer inertia of the majority concerned. The brave movement petered out; and the locusts were to consume many more years before the recommendations of the Committee of Inquiry were taken up again.

So the rival Books, Green and Red, staggered on towards their inevitable doom. Early in 1829 the Underwriters felt under the necessity to raise the price of their book from eight to ten guineas, admitting that it had been running at an annual loss of £500 for 20 years past, and that the value of the Stock which guaranteed its appearance had dwindled from £12,000 to £2,000. They added that some 10,000 vessels were surveyed every year, and that the salaries of surveyors could not possibly be reduced. Since the two Principal Surveyors in London were then receiving £250 a year between them the latter warning can be said to have rested on solid ground.

Otherwise, this notice is of much historical interest in being headed "Lloyd's Registry of Shipping", the first use of the proper name in this context.

All branches of the shipping community were thus brought to contemplate with alarm the possible consequences of a deadlock. The Napoleonic Wars were long over. The trading monopoly of the East India Company was broken in 1833. Canada and the new United States were opening up to trade. The British opportunity of becoming the most powerful maritime nation in the world was as the most glorious dawn commercial man had ever seen. The wealth and power of the City of London, so much concerned with the ownership and insurance of shipping, and with the handling of exports and imports, demanded imperatively the organised classification and registration of the country's carriers by sea.

This time, the first move towards breaking the deadlock came from Lloyd's itself. During the summer of 1833 its leading figures set up a Sub-Committee to confer with the Committees of the Green and Red Books—and it will be noted that the Underwriters' Register had, by implication, already become to be regarded, however subtly, as something apart from Lloyd's proper. A meeting of the parties was thus arranged for August 14th, to be held in the Merchant Seamen's Office, and this got down to serious business promptly, as is shewn in a minute still extant. The gathering was attended by five representatives of the Red Book, six of the Green, with five delegates from the Corporation of Lloyd's proper. After prolonged discussion two resolutions were unanimously passed, thus:—

> "1st. That it is not practicable to carry on two Register Books as at present circumstanced.
> "2nd. That in the opinion of this meeting it is desirable that an union of the Committees of the two Registers take place for the purpose of establishing one good and efficient Register."

The details of the subsequent negotiations are of little interest now, for there was no effective opposition to the merger, and pride and prejudice were at last seen to be irrelevant. A meeting of the Committee of the two Registries, held at the River Dee offices over the Royal Exchange on October 10th, 1833, appointed a Joint Committee to carry the proposed union into effect. This in turn appointed a sub-committee of seven members to go into the details of the reorganisation; and the seven worked so promptly that a draft outline of a proposed Constitution and of working arrangements was ready for the approval of the full Joint Committee on October 24th. So the meetings went on until, near the end of the year, there was formed a Provisional Committee of "the new Society", to manage its affairs until October, 1834—the first wholly unified authority. The Green and Red Books were to be wound up in December, 1833.

What, then, of the new scheme in detail?

First of all, the recommendations of the 1824–26 Committee of Inquiry were adopted with only a few alterations. Surveyors to the new Society were to be whole-time officers, devoting themselves exclusively to the Society's business. The most important clause of all ran:—

> "That the characters to be assigned shall be, as nearly as circumstances will permit, a correct indication of the real and intrinsic quality of the ship; and that the same shall no longer be regulated, as heretofore, by the incorrect standard of the port of building nor on the decision of the Surveyors; but will henceforward be in all cases finally affixed by the Committee, after due inspection of the Reports of the Surveyors and the documents which may be submitted to them."

With regard to the constitution of the new Society, there were to be 24 members of the governing body, eight each from among the Merchants, the Shipowners and the Underwriters. The Chairman of Lloyd's and the Chairman of the General Shipowners' Society were to be members *ex officio*. Six members were to retire annually, two of each group, to be replaced or re-elected from within that group.

The financial aspects of the scheme were gone into with the thoroughness proper to the City of London. It was ascertained at once that very little could be expected of the Government beyond hearty good wishes. Whitehall declined even to sanction any abatement of the then heavy postal fees on the transmission of surveyors' reports from the outports; its best was to offer through the Board of Trade a list of all ships of over 50 tons registered in the United Kingdom and the Colonies.

Even so, careful estimates convinced the promoters that the new Book could be sold to subscribers for three guineas annually and at ten guineas to what were elegantly called "Public Establishments"—the funds fortified by charges to be levied on shipowners for survey and classification in accordance with a scale based on tonnage. The four marine insurance companies in London—the Royal Exchange, London, Alliance and Mutual Indemnity—had already agreed to give an annual subscription of 100 guineas each. More than that, Lloyd's as a body put up £1,000 to get the venture started, and individual underwriters contributed more than £700. It is of much interest that the advance of £1,000 from Lloyd's was repaid within a few years.

The summer of 1834 was a frantically busy time for the members of the Provisional Committee. They met daily; and in September they met three times in one day, at 11 a.m., 4 p.m., and 7 p.m. At length, on the anniversary of Trafalgar, October 21st, 1834, the Provisional Committee dissolved and handed over to the Permanent Committee of *Lloyd's Register of British and Foreign Shipping*.

The names of those who constituted the first Permanent Committee of Lloyd's Register of British and Foreign Shipping, a list of historical importance, were:—

Merchants

(Appointed by the Provisional Committee)

J. W. Buckle	Crawford D. Kerr
T. A. Curtis	George Lyall, M.P.
Thomson Hankey, Jr.	Alexander Mitchell
George Hanson	Patrick M. Stewart, M.P.

Shipowners

(Elected by the Committee of the General Shipowners' Society)

Thomas Benson	Joseph Somes
Nathaniel Domett	William Tindall
Richard Drew	Thomas Ward
B. A. McGhie	George F. Young, M.P.

Underwriters

(Elected by the Committee of Lloyd's)

George Allfrey	William Marshall
David Carruthers	John Robinson
Thomas Chapman	R. H. Shepard
Henry Cheape	Arthur Willis

Chairman of Lloyd's

George R. Robinson, M.P.

Chairman of the General Shipowners' Society

Octavius Wigram

The retention of Lloyd's name may seem a little surprising, and it was not relished by some of the shipowners, who not unreasonably felt that they had suffered a good deal at the hands of the underwriters. It was also disapproved by more detached persons who felt that the use of the name would suggest a predominance of the underwriting interests. The choice was a wise one, as sensible men soon came to realise. It gave the new venture the prestige that Lloyd's had earned in international regard; and Lloyd's Register was quickly to enhance the importance of the name inherited from the Welshman who kept a coffee house in Abchurch Lane.

The new Register had then to find headquarters and a permanent staff. The Provisional Committee had used the board room of the General Shipowners' Society at No. 72, Cornhill, and the prospectus of the joint venture was in fact issued from that address. Several modest premises were inspected—and, considering the small resources available, modest they had to be.

Eventually a place at No. 2, White Lion Court, Cornhill, was taken at an inclusive rental of £175. This consisted of two rooms on the first floor, two on the second and one on the upper storey. It housed on the first floor and the upper storey the staff of Secretary, the three London surveyors, two clerks, two "posters" of the Register Books and one messenger. The second floor was reconstructed to provide an adequate board room for the Committee who, it will be recalled, alone had power to issue certificates of classification—though this task was delegated in 1837 to a Sub-Committee for Classification.

The first Secretary was Mr. Nathaniel Symonds, who had acted as such for the Shipowners' Society. He was succeeded in January, 1837, by Mr. Charles Graham from the Admiralty clerical staff. The Senior Clerk was Mr. Henry Adams, who, before his death in 1887, had put in 72 years of service with Lloyd's Register, first with the Underwriters' Register from 1815, and latterly as Chief Clerk to the new authority.

Lloyd's Register of British and Foreign Shipping was thus firmly established, 74 years after its first formal appearance and after 35 years of wasteful competition between the Green and Red Books. And that conflict was not to be by any means the last of the little wars in which even the reorganised Register was to be involved.

CHAPTER 3   GROWING PAINS

THE story of Lloyd's Register between 1760 and 1834 is so packed
with differences and disputes at the highest level, one may very well
wonder how the men charged with the practical tasks of ship survey
fared during the years of controversy. That they were grossly under-
paid we know, and we may surmise that they suffered from a sense of
insecurity, whether employed by the Underwriters or the Shipowners.

We know next to nothing about the sort of men they were. We can
only surmise that they were mostly retired master mariners, veteran
craftsmen in shipbuilding, and the like. It is a fair assumption that
none had any formal training in the technique and mathematics of
naval architecture, such as a third-year apprentice would have to-day.
We may nevertheless be sure that they were shrewd men, "skeely
skippers", who knew a good ship when they saw one, even if their only

test of the soundness of timber was to stick the blade of a knife into a bulkhead.

The first surveyor mentioned by name in early records was a Mr. Thomas Whitewood, whose survey was referred to in a legal action brought by the owners of the *Mills Frigate* against the underwriters in 1764. Another, Mr. Alexander Stupart, is mentioned in the Book of 1781–82 as having been appointed to undertake surveys of damaged vessels to be repaired "in the River of Thames". A careful analysis of the first of the surviving Books indicates that, about 1766, there were 15 surveying ports—London, Liverpool, Hull, Leith, Poole, Cowes, Topsham, Whitehaven, Exeter, Lynn, Teignmouth, Weymouth, Yarmouth, Portsmouth and Star Cross, in approximately that order of importance . . . and how many of us to-day could off-hand say exactly where all these places are to be found? By 1781 the number of surveying ports had risen to 23, but it appears to be almost certain that the strength of the regular surveying staff was not equal to that.

The historian must forever lament the loss of those early documents that probably went up in the flames of the Royal Exchange in February, 1838. The establishment of the new Register, however, provided a fresh starting-point. We know now that, from 1834, the Society started with a carefully appointed staff of 63 surveyors. Thirteen of these were exclusively servants of the Committee—three stationed in London, two each at Liverpool, Sunderland and Hull, and one each at Bristol, Glasgow, Leith and Newcastle. The remaining 50 were classed as non-exclusive surveyors, part-time representatives in outlying ports, their work subject to the supervision of the exclusive officers.

This considerable body of surveyors was then sub-divided into two classes—the shipwright surveyors and the nautical surveyors: a curious but important distinction. The shipwright surveyors were those who had served a proper apprenticeship in the crafts of ship-building, while the nautical surveyors were experienced shipmasters with a knowledge of the construction and repair of vessels. Officers of the former class appear to have concentrated on the oversight of new vessels on the stocks, while the latter surveyed vessels afloat. Men of both classes joined in surveys of older ships in drydock wherever that was feasible. Clearly, this rather elaborate system amply provided for the upgrading of those vessels which, having dropped out of their original classification by reason of age, had been sufficiently overhauled and repaired to justify their reinstatement.

The surveyors were paid well by the standards of the period. The shipwright surveyor in London received £500 per annum, while, at the other end of the scale, the nautical surveyors at Bristol, Glasgow and Leith got £150. Each non-exclusive surveyor received a retaining fee of some £20 a year, with a percentage of the fees received by the parent body for their work. Within the new dispensation, therefore, the prime importance of the surveying branch was fully recognised. Whereas the business of survey cost about £4,000 per annum, head office was run at rather less than £2,000—and that included the costs of printing and posting the Register Books. It is pleasant to know that the administrative costs included an annual charge of £170 for the services of two watermen and two apprentices for the conveyance of surveyors among the ships in the Thames and in the London Docks. These worthies were provided each year with a brand new jacket and badge, the latter engraved with the name of the Society.

The re-formed Society thus appears to have been soundly organised for its job, but some time was to pass before the fruits of re-organisation could be harvested. Indeed, the new Register Book, issued in 1834, was rather a makeshift production. The Green Book of 1833 had contained the names of 16,615 vessels, the Red Book of the same year those of 15,670. The first volume of the new Book listed only 12,847 vessels, whether classed or not. The last issues of the earlier Books, however, had included the names of some 3,000 foreign vessels trading to British ports; and the apparently incomplete nature of the first issue of the new Book was due mainly to the fact that the lately-appointed staff had to begin with a set of figures supplied by the Commissioners of Custom. Then they had to start from scratch on the task of re-surveying practically the whole of the Merchant Navy of Britain in accordance with new Rules, to the formation of which the reconstituted Society now addressed itself.

It took about five years to complete this work. Within that period 15,000 vessels were surveyed, each report carefully dealt with by the unpaid Committee. Ships for which classification had never been sought were dropped from the issue for 1838, and yet the bulk of the Book was as considerable as ever it had been. As its authority grew, the Committee took upon itself something like disciplinary powers.

Any new vessel for which an A1 classification was sought must undergo "a survey under construction", which meant in effect that its progress was closely inspected at least three times while the hull was on the stocks. If this condition was not met, then one year was deducted from the period during which it might remain in its allotted class; and these penalties were stiffened as time went on.

Four different classifications were now the rule, based substantially on the recommendations of the 1824–26 Committee of Inquiry. These were:—

> "The letter A indicated the first description of the First Class, including ships that had not passed a prescribed age and had been kept in the highest state of repair and efficiency.
>
> "The diphthong Æ denoted the second description of the First Class, and applied to vessels which had passed the prescribed age, and had not undergone the repairs required for continuation or restoration to the A character, but were still considered fit for the safe conveyance of dry and perishable cargoes.
>
> "The letter E, designated the Second Class, comprised ships which, although unfit for carrying dry cargoes, were considered perfectly safe for the conveyance to all parts of the world of cargoes not in their nature liable to sea damage.
>
> "The Third Class, denoted by the letter I, included vessels which were good in constitution and fit for the conveyance on short voyages (not out of Europe) of cargoes not subject to sea damage.
>
> "The condition of the anchors, cables and stores, when satisfactory, was indicated by the figure 1; and when unsatisfactory, by the figure 2."

One change was made in 1837 with the introduction of a new class designated *Æ in *red*, this to represent vessels of a class slightly superior to those in older Æ category. At the same time, conditions for the maintenance of ships in the A class were slightly eased; and into the Rules were introduced new tables, specifying more closely than before the classification of a vessel according to the different kinds of wood that had been put into its construction.

So the new Register meant business, favouring a more and more scientific approach to the business of ship surveying. And it was not long before some among the shipowners, even on the Committee, were murmuring their fears that their old antagonists, the underwriters, were overdoing the stringency in their own sectional interests. In this inner conflict shipbuilders inclined to side with shipowners, merchants with underwriters. The infant Register was not firmly on its feet until it had survived quite a number of teething troubles.

*   *   *   *   *

Despite the thought and energy and goodwill that had been put into the drafting of the new Rules, the Book failed to prosper immediately and in fact looked for a time in a fair way to turn out a disastrous failure. The number of subscribers to the original edition of 1834 was 721, but this dwindled within two years to 615. As the Christmas of 1836 approached the funds had shrunk so alarmingly that the Chairman of the Society, Mr. Thomas Chapman, had to advance a sum of his own money to ensure that the officers should have their salaries in time for the festive season.

More than one factor contributed to the slowness of the start. The shipping community as a whole had been disillusioned by the fecklessness of the struggle between the Green and the Red Books. There was always the inherent British prejudice against novelty. The latent conflict between shipowners and underwriters weakened the foundations of trust; and other parties than the shipowners and shipbuilders felt that the Society was going too far and fast in its strict and, in some eyes, arbitrary requirements. British trade in general was, moreover, passing through a bad spell.

The first open, and serious, revolt against the authority of the new Register, however, sprang from that persistent tendency in British affairs: the revolt of what are called the Provinces against the domination of London.

This revolt really started among the tough men of Sunderland, then as now a vital base of British shipbuilding power. The outports were quick to realise that, while the constitution of the new Society provided amply for representation of all branches of the shipping industry, the representatives were drawn from the shipping community of London alone. The first prospectus had been eloquent about their "earnest desire to cultivate and maintain the most perfect good understanding with the merchants, shipowners and underwriters of the different ports of the United Kingdom, on whose support and co-operation they rely for the promotion of the objects of the Institution, within their respective districts," and there is no doubt that they often went to commercial bodies at the outports for advice and assistance. No sooner had the prospectus of 1834 been published, however, than the Committee heard the first rumbles of protest from Sunderland. They were then immediately faced with direct action from Liverpool.

The Liverpool objections were in the first place against the proposed scale of charges for survey. This was followed by the suggestion that a local Committee should be set up in affiliation with the Committee in London. The Society rejected this notion on the ground that the powers demanded by the men of Merseyside were greater than the Constitution of the Society allowed. Negotiations broke down; and in 1835 there appeared the "Liverpool Register of Shipping".

This work of reference listed only vessels belonging to Liverpool or trading regularly in and out of the Mersey. It made no attempt at classification. Only one issue appears to have seen the light of day. But it was a straw that showed the way certain winds were blowing during that clouded decade of the Reform Bill and trade depression.

The constitution and workings of Lloyd's Register of British and Foreign Shipping became subjects of discussion in newspapers throughout the country, and it was occasionally bitter enough to trouble the Society in London. An attempt to quieten the atmosphere was entrusted to the General Shipowners' Society. This body was given the unprecedented right of electing one-half of the members of the Register Committee, and it proceeded to see that representatives of the outports were elected as vacancies occurred. Thus, in one year, out of the 12 persons returned by the Shipowners' Society to serve on the Committee of Lloyd's Register, five were the nominees of outports—Whitby, Sunderland, Scarborough, South Shields and North Shields.

In considering these movements one should always have in mind the difficulty of internal communications at that period of time. There were no comfortable night trains to carry a delegate from, say, Glasgow to London in less than eight hours, no aircraft to cover the distance in less than two hours. The concentration of control in London was logistically inevitable. Even so, that was not enough for Liverpool. In 1838 the merchants and shipowners of that city raised a guarantee fund and created a separate Register of their own. The new "Liverpool Register of Shipping" closely imitated Lloyd's Register in symbols of classification and even in the working of the Rules.

Its life was short. Whatever the reasons, the proposal to return to the fold came from the rebellious Liverpool Committee in 1844. It did not, however, come on hands and knees. Liverpool agreed that it was desirable to have only one Book for the whole of the United Kingdom, but it suggested that two Boards of Management should be approved, that at Liverpool to have sole control within its own district, London to continue to look after itself and the rest of the country.

One may fairly feel that the Liverpudlians were in this getting a little above themselves, and Lloyd's Register would have none of it. It was conceded, however, that a Sub-Committee should look into proposed amendments of the Rules; and, to cut a long and not very interesting story short, an agreement was reached on April 28th, 1845. Liverpool returned to the fold, but the particulars of vessels classed by the local committee were to be printed in an appendix to Lloyd's Register for a year or two thereafter.

The Liverpool revolt, however, was not by any means without its considerable consequences. London conceded that there should be a Liverpool Branch Committee of 12 members, fully representative of all branches of the shipping industry in the city: the first of its kind outside London. The Chairman and Deputy-Chairman of this body, along with the Chairman of the local Classification Committee, were to be *ex officio* members of the London Committee. The Branch Committee would continue to have a say in the classification of vessels surveyed in the Liverpool district.

This was, as the worn but useful phrase goes, the thin end of the wedge. While the general sovereignty of Lloyd's Register in the matter of classification was recognised, London had been forced for the first time to make considerable concessions to one of the larger outports.

The fact remains that the original Lloyd's Register survived. The early criticisms and the revolt of Liverpool were directed against a Book which could only be experimental after the fusion of 1834. Liverpool's ultimate approach to London ten years later was an admission that the position of Lloyd's Book, its early imperfections removed and the fresh survey of British shipping proceeding apace, was not to be seriously shaken. Its authority was being acknowledged more and more widely, and that in ways the general public could begin to understand.

The Annual Report of the General Shipowners' Society for 1840—this from a body naturally sensitive about its own interests as against those of underwriters and merchants—spoke out handsomely:—

> "The last point to which your Committee would especially call attention is one which involves probably a greater degree of real importance than any other charge entrusted to their superintendence. It is the position occupied by the Committee in relation to the now really national establishment of *Lloyd's Register of British and Foreign Shipping*. The vast influence over the shipping property of the country exercised by that Committee, though by some imperfectly understood, and by many inadequately estimated, may be inferred from the fact that 11,595 ships and vessels are now recorded in the Register . . .
>
> "It is the unhesitating belief of your Committee that, making reasonable allowance for difficulties inseparable from such a task, this important duty is, on the whole, ably, impartially, and beneficially performed; the general character of British Shipping having considerably improved since the establishment of the new system."

The compliment was repeated in a still more public way in the proceedings of a Select Committee of the House of Commons, convened in 1843 to consider the subject of shipwrecks, of which the frequency had begun to agitate popular opinion. The *Shipping and Mercantile Gazette*, a lively critic of the new Book in its early days, went out of its way about the same time to admit that the Committee of Lloyd's Register had "exercised their functions with honour, firmness and impartiality", going on to declare that the Register had "acquired so great an importance as an authority upon the value and seaworthiness of merchant vessels, that it would be impossible for ever so good a ship to obtain freight abroad without reference to the Register".

The year of grace, 1845, when the collapse of the Liverpool Register left it alone in the field, can thus be regarded as one of the vital dates in the history of Lloyd's Register. Two years earlier, more than 12,000 British ships had been classified, more than one-half of these carrying the highest classification, A1. The aggregate amount of shipping classed was in the region of 2,500,000 tons, more than two-thirds of the total of the British Merchant Marine.

It is a pleasant domestic illustration of the increasing activity and strength of the Society that, in 1848, the Committee took from the Merchant Taylors' Company a new lease of the whole of the premises at No. 2, White Lion Court, while the "posters" of the Register Book —a band of functionaries in the year 1960 sadly dwindled in numbers, but of whom we shall hear more later on—were separately accommodated in a room at No. 77, Cornhill, near at hand.

CHAPTER 4   IRON AND STEAM

THE reader of this History in 1960 may require to be reminded
that, for the first 80 years or so of its existence, Lloyd's Register in
its various forms was concerned entirely with sailing vessels built of
wood. It is a reasonable surmise that, if the Committee in London
had several brushes with the outports and seemed occasionally to be
stubborn and conservative, that was mainly because they continued
long to think of shipping in terms of wood and canvas while the banks
of the northern rivers—notably the Wear, the Tyne and the Clyde—
were on fire with the exciting promises of iron and steam.

The inclination of London towards the older techniques was
wholly natural and completely admirable. It upheld, however
unconsciously, the sturdy English tradition of the wooden walls that,
built in southern ports, had saved England from the Armada and

D

Britain from Napoleon. The craft of wooden shipbuilding was ancient, beautiful, efficient in its day, and the seamanship that went to handling its products was superb.

The Thames was still a great shipbuilding river. As we have seen, the more powerful shipowners about the turn of the century were in London and could pay the best prices for the best ships. James Watt and Henry Bell and those other clever fellows in the far North were playing with fire, their experiments as yet unproven. Southern England had found that the wooden sailing ship worked, and that it was there-fore—in the line of practical thought that has served the English so well—a good thing. Probably the mercantile shipping men of that period regarded Nelson's *Victory* as a bag of mechanical tricks, with its special gear for hoisting monstrous sails, swinging heavy yards, raising enormous anchors and moving ammunition. One wonders what they could have thought of a *Queen Mary*, even of a modern cargo liner, with so many mechanical things in its inner parts, quite apart from the propelling machinery, that it carries more engineer than deck officers.

The early records contain just a few notations that we can regard as mildly amusing now. A novelty of 1813 or thereabouts was the introduction of iron cables for mooring purposes—that is, in place of hempen hawsers. The Underwriters' Register of that year acknowledged the innovation by granting vessels thus equipped the notation of "Iron Cable" against their names; and the Book of 1816 added the letters "P.I.C." to denote that such cables had been proved by test. In a note to the Green Book it was stated that, in the case of a vessel fitted with iron cables to the exclusion of hemp, the figure denoting the quality of equipment was omitted—presumably, though the clause is ambiguous, because a ship fitted with iron cables was equipped in a first class way. It will be seen later on that chains and cables were to provoke serious issues for the Society, even for Parliament.

Just a decade later there broke out a small controversy as to the best manner of sheathing the bottom of a ship to protect it against fouling and the Teredo worm. In 1820 one entry in the Green Book mentions that the ship concerned was "sheathed with zinc", while another, in 1831, surprisingly describes a hull as being "sheathed with tanned leather". All manner of experiments were made to find some sort of protection against the development of fouling on timber continually exposed to the action of sea water. Speculative men experimented with treatment by sulphate of copper, sulphate of iron, creosote and so on. It was concluded in the long run that nothing was better for the preservation of a ship's timbers than applications of rock salt: even to the extent of boiling the wood in salt water before it was worked into shape.

The major shipping event of the early 19th Century, however, was the advent of steam propulsion. This was the event that was to force the South of England away from its preoccupation with the wooden sailing ship, ultimately to rob the Thames of its predominance in shipbuilding and, more to our present purpose, vastly to widen the scope of Lloyd's Register of Shipping and increase its responsibilities of survey and inspection.

The history of the application of steam power to man's purposes is long and hopelessly befogged by romantic legends. The most misleading of these is that James Watt, having watched the play of steam on the lid of his mother's kettle as a child, "invented the steam engine". Many children born long before Watt had wondered at the lifting of the kettle lid, and quite a number of men had constructed steam engines of a sort. The trouble with these was that they would not work efficiently; and the triumph of Watt— a Greenock lad then employed as a mechanic in Glasgow University—was to hit on the notion of the separate condenser whereby it became possible to create a vacuum and use the steam expansively in the cylinder. Throughout his long life, nobly backed by Matthew Boulton of Birmingham, Watt was to improve the application of steam power in many ways, but his prime discovery was that separate condenser, which made the steam engine a practical and economic proposition.

The history of the application of steam power to the propulsion of ships has been equally confused by romantic historians. At least a dozen inventive men in Spain, France, England and America made efforts to bring the miracle about, even as early as the 16th Century. Some of these experiments broke down because their authors could not, like "Jonathan Hulls with his patent sculls", envisage the right means of connecting the power unit with the water. When, however, Watt's discovery of the principle of the separate condenser turned the steam engine into something that really worked, the men interested in the application of steam power to the propulsion of ships had something solid to go on. The rest was the problem of so gearing the power unit to its extensions in the water that a vessel could be pushed forward at steady speed. How to make it go backwards was quite another question.

Out of the welter of evidence it emerges with tolerable certainty that the first man to get a boat moving steadily over water was William Symington, a mechanic in the still remote village of Wanlockhead, Dumfries-shire: one of those grave, speculative Scotsmen who are engineers born rather than made. He had already earned a small reputation for himself with a sort of steam carriage when, in 1788, he was commissioned to engine a steam-boat for the somewhat eccentric Patrick Miller, a well-to-do Edinburgh banker and landowner. This little vessel, only 25 feet in length, was launched and started on the lake within Miller's estate at Dalswinton, Dumfriesshire, making a speed of five miles an hour before a concourse of invited guests, including the poet, Robert Burns. It is of much technical interest that Symington's first boat was a twin-hulled job with the paddles between the hulls.

Miller nearly bankrupted himself through his experiments, but Symington had another chance 12 years later, when Lord Dundas of Kerse financed him to produce a steam-boat for use on the Forth and Clyde Canal. This small vessel, the *Charlotte Dundas*, is described by most authorities as the "first practically successful steam-boat ever built." Engined by one of James Watt's double-acting jobs, coupled by crank and connecting rod to a stern-wheel, on her trial in March, 1802, she towed two laden barges, each of 70 tons burden, over a stretch of 20 miles in six hours, and that against a strong headwind. Unfortunately, the authorities decided that the wash from this early steamer must damage the canal banks, and the *Charlotte Dundas* was beached in a backwater.

Symington's last days were passed unhappily in London. He was taken up by that great enthusiast of canals, the second Earl of Bridgwater, and commissioned to build six steam-boats for work on the inland waterways, but the nobleman died untimely, and poor Symington passed his last years on the charity of relations. He lies in an unmarked grave in the churchyard of St. Botolph's, Aldgate, but the Institute of Marine Engineers saw to the placing of a memorial tablet within the church.

But still the *Charlotte Dundas* lay rotting on the banks of the Forth and Clyde Canal, her mechanical equipment there for all who cared to study it. She was certainly inspected by a man called Henry Bell; she may have been looked at by the American, Robert Fulton. It is known that Bell and Fulton corresponded on the techniques of steam propulsion, both of them enthusiasts of the new science. In August, 1807, Fulton put into service on the Hudson River the steam vessel *Clermont*, 133 feet in length and powered by an engine out of the Boulton & Watt works at Birmingham. She covered the 142-mile stretch between New York and Albany in 32 hours steaming time, and she went on successfully to be beyond any doubt "the first steam-boat profitably employed." In 1812, Henry Bell, who had been trained as a millwright in his native Linlithgow, put into the Clyde the little *Comet* to ply from Glasgow to Greenock and across the Firth to Helensburgh, where he kept an hotel—certainly the first steam-boat profitably employed on this side of the Atlantic.

Wherever the credit lies—and many historians give most of it to Symington—the appearance of the *Comet* was a great event in the world's maritime history, and its consequences became of profound concern to the Committee of Lloyd's Register. It was not merely that the classification of steam-driven vessels created new problems for the surveyors. The location of the new industry along the banks of the northern rivers inflamed once more the slumbering rivalry between the outports on the one hand and the conservative body in London on the other. We see now that the Society was rather backward in appreciating the implications of mechanisation and in adjusting itself to the inevitable.

The first steam-driven vessel mentioned in the Register was the *James Watt* and that in a supplement to the Green Book for 1822. Her hull, 124 feet in length, was built by that John Wood of Port Glasgow who had built the *Comet* and many other early steam-boats, and she was driven by a Boulton & Watt engine of 100 horse power. Classed A1, this ship was to play a dumb part in literary history. When the ailing Sir Walter Scott was brought home from the Mediterranean in one of H.M. ships, to London, and after he had lain for three weeks in rooms in Jermyn Street, it was decided that he had best be taken home to Abbotsford by sea. The vessel selected was this *James Watt*, which was being employed by the London, Leith and Edinburgh Shipping Company on the East Coast route.

This sort of coastal voyage was popular until the railways developed, and those sufficiently curious will find in *The Steam-Boat*, by Scott's contemporary as a novelist, John Galt, some remarkably vivid renderings of the nature and "atmosphere" of travel in those primitive craft.

The appearance of this steam-boat in the Register was soon followed by other entries of the kind. The Green Book for 1827 contained the names of 81 steamers, that for 1832 a round 100. Among these was the *Enterprise*, the first steam-driven vessel to accomplish the voyage to India under power. This ship was built in London, the fact suggesting that the shipbuilders of the southern river had taken to the new-fangled machinery at an early stage, but the conclusion is unsound. Hereabouts it is important to understand the position of the shipbuilding business of that distant period in relation to the steam engine.

The shipbuilder and the engineer of the 1830's were craftsmen with quite different outlooks and not, as so often nowadays, one and the same thing. The engineer was, roughly speaking, the bustling pioneer, and when he wished to try out one of his products, he went to the more conservative shipbuilder to provide him with a suitable hull for his infernal machine. Those early hulls were all of wood. Even if they were built unusually strong to take the weight and thrusts of engines, they were still the work of conventional craftsmen who built ships according to the traditional rules applicable to sail. The evidence is scanty, but it appears that when Lloyd's Register granted an A1 classification to an early steam-boat, the certificate of excellence applied to the wooden hull alone. The ultimate fusion of engine and hull for classification purposes was, as we shall see, the outcome of a major crisis in the evolution of the modern steamship.

The gradual nature of that evolution cannot be over-emphasised. There was never an abrupt end of one phase and then a glorious new start of another in shipbuilding practice. The side-paddle for the propulsion of steam vessels was not suddenly dropped when the higher efficiency of the propeller was decisively proved. Many ship-owners were slow to discard sails after their vessels had been engined. Some of the loveliest and fastest sailing ships were built in the 1860's when the all-round superiority of steam had already been demonstrated. A very large sailing vessel, the *Archibald Russell*, was built by Scott's of Greenock as late as 1905, and the *Pamir*, which met disaster in late 1957, reminded us all that the full-rigged ship has still its limited uses.

If Lloyd's Register was in any degree tardy in recognising the importance of steam, that was only a reflection of the slowness of the evolutionary process. The new Book of 1834 did, it is true, recognise the approach of the age of steam, but its reference to steamers was brief, and the Rules did not provide for the survey of machinery by appointed officers of Lloyd's Register. Roughly, they followed the Government regulation already in force, requiring surveys to be held twice a year, a competent Master Engineer to issue a certificate regarding the condition of engines and boilers. If the report was satisfactory, the vessel was assigned the notation MC in the Register Book—that is, Machinery Certified—but that was hardly classification in the full sense of the term.

The Government regulation had sprung out of an Inquiry held as early as 1817. Public opinion had been much disturbed by the frequency of boiler explosions in the new-fangled ships, and the Board of Trade ultimately ruled that all steam-boats must be registered; that boilers, which must be of wrought iron or copper, should be open to inspection; and that every boiler should be fitted with two safety valves and tested to three times the working pressure. Those sufficiently interested in these remote matters will find in the gracious shadows of Paisley Abbey a quaint but pathetic memorial to the victims of an explosion on board the steam-boat *Earl Grey* in 1835 at Greenock—the birthplace of James Watt, by a small irony of history.

*   *   *   *   *

If the Committee and surveyors of Lloyd's Register were thus indecisive in their handling of the problems presented by the development of the steam engine, they were to be sorely troubled by those raised through the increasing use of iron instead of wood in the construction of ships' hulls.

This was a revolution. The period between 1820 and 1860 was one of such violent transition in the world of shipbuilding and engineering that even the best brains within the industry hesitated to lay down laws as to the evolution of shipping in general. The change from sail-and-wood to steam-and-iron was seismic in eventual effect, but the process was long drawn out in time, with innumerable overlappings of custom and novelty, of old and new practices. It is not at all surprising that the Committee and surveyors of Lloyd's Register, long habituated to practice in sailing ships with wooden hulls, were taken off-balance when the shipbuilders increasingly inclined to the use of metals.

They had had plenty of warning, to be sure. Even the hearts of oak who sailed and fought the wooden walls at Trafalgar knew that a hull made of iron would not sink of its own weight. Iron barges had been built at Cartmel in North Lancashire and used on the inland waterways in the 1780's. Iron boats were being built on a branch of the Forth and Clyde Canal in 1818 and at Birkenhead in 1829 by John Laird, founder of the great firm of Cammell Laird & Co. The first iron vessel driven by a steam engine was the *Aaron Manby*, built at the Horsely Ironworks, Tipton, in 1820–21. The Clyde followed with the *Aglaia* in 1832, the Tyne with the *Prince Albert* in the same year.

The first that Lloyd's Register heard of iron ships officially was through their local surveyors in Liverpool, in October, 1836. This concerned a ketch built by Messrs. Fawcett for steam dredging in the Bay of Tunis—the *Goliath* of 77 tons. The owners did not seek to have this craft classified, but "merely wished for a report thereon to be sent to London in order that the Broker, or parties applied to underwrite her, might have access to it". The Committee obliged by recording this vessel's particulars in the Register Book without classification; her name appears in a supplement to the 1836 Book, with the bleak notation, "Built of Iron," against it.

In 1837 the sizeable iron ship *Sirius*, built at Millwall by Fairbairn & Co. under the inspection of the London surveyors of the Society, was allowed the A1 classification without any terms of years stated. A year later the iron sailing ship *Ironside*, built by Jackson & Jordan of Liverpool under survey, was registered, but again without classification and with only the notation "Built of Iron". The case of the *Ironside* is specially interesting, if only because Professor Airy of the Royal Observatory at Greenwich—afterwards Sir George Airy, Astronomer Royal—was called in by the builders to suggest means of counteracting the local effect of iron plates on the ship's compasses.

This was all very unsatisfactory. The Committee in London was clearly confused by the several implications of the new methods of construction and propulsion. They fell into the habit of assigning vessels of the more advanced types to vague lists of "Ships built of Iron" or "Ships navigated by Steam". They were still far from exactly classifying an iron steamer as a unit, hull and engines in one.

Whether they liked or not, however, the number of iron steamships rapidly increased, to the extent that, in 1844, the Committee appealed to the shipbuilders of Britain for co-operation in compiling such Rules for the survey and classification of iron steamers as, they had been assured, were wanted by the shipping community in general.

The response was disheartening. It was made clear at once that the shipowners and shipbuilders alike were just as sadly lost as the Society among the imponderables of the new sciences. As one looks back on that period from the vantage point of 1960, the situation in 1840 seems to have been much as it is in the field of aeronautics today, when a variety of methods of propulsion and designs of aircraft are the matter of vivid technical discussion and often acute difference. The climate of feeling was best expressed by Robert Napier, the father-figure of shipbuilding in its engineering aspects, and a man who did not speak without weighing his words. His reply to the Committee's circular ran thus:—

> "I have, like your Committee, the most earnest desire to see Iron Ships built on the strongest and most scientific principles. I am very sorry at being under the necessity of stating that I cannot see any way of filling up your Questionnaire satisfactorily, as I consider the subject so involved with practical difficulties that it would be impossible to make Rules to meet the different cases honestly, and so as not to do much injury to this new and growing branch of shipbuilding and trade."

Other iron shipbuilders on the Clyde, the Tyne and the Thames replied to much the same effect. All that the Committee of Lloyd's Register could do in these circumstances was to invite shipbuilders to submit specifications of new ships before construction started, these to be considered in the light of such experience as had already been accumulated; and this scheme was successful up to a point.

The output of iron ships went on increasing, however, and with increasing rapidity. Indeed, something like a state of anarchy developed within the iron shipbuilding industry during the 1850's—the decade that saw Britain vaunt its industrial progress in the Great Exhibition. Scientific men had been given their heads. New ideas proliferated so widely and wildly that the different shipbuilding districts in the North were each apt to be working along diverging lines of development and so hostile towards each other.

This was not a happy situation for an institution pledged to maintain standards and assign accurate classifications, and in 1853 the Society appointed a Sub-Committee to consider the situation and report with a view to formulating those Rules for Iron Ships which, despite the differences within the shipbuilding industry, were still demanded by the shipping community as a whole.

The Society's Principal Surveyors, J. Martin and J. H. Ritchie, toured the most important iron shipyards throughout the kingdom; the experience gained by the outport surveyors was assembled and collated. At a conference at Glasgow in February, 1854—note the significance of the place of meeting—a first set of Rules was drafted. These were closely scanned and slightly amended by both the Liverpool and the General Committees, and there appeared in the Register Book for 1855 the first "Rules for Iron Ships" issued by the Society.

According to these Rules, iron ships built under survey could be classed for periods of six, nine and twelve years, subject to occasional and annual surveys as practicable and to special survey in drydock or on blocks every third year. The Society's note on the general subject, however, admits a certain degree of uneasiness, thus:—

> "Considering that Iron Shipbuilding is yet in its infancy, and that there are no well-understood general rules for building Iron Ships, the Committee have not deemed it desirable to frame a scheme compelling the adoption of a particular form or mode of construction; but that certain general requirements should be put forward having for their basis the thickness of plates and substance of frames, showing a *minimum in each particular*, to entitle ships to the character A for a period of years, subject, however, to certain periodical surveys; and also to a continuation of such character, should their state and condition justify it on subsequent examination."

These first definite Rules for Iron Ships, slightly expanded in 1857, served for a period of about ten years, but not with complete satisfaction to all parties. The theories and practices of the advanced iron shipbuilders continued to conflict. Nobody had shown with certainty, for instance, how the continuous action of sea water tended to affect metal surfaces or how certain types of cargo might be affected by chemical emanations within iron holds. Some designers held that the new Rules required material greatly in excess of what was necessary, and the designers were continually running ahead with notions far beyond those contemplated in the draft regulations of 1854: so swift was progress in this field.

The Committee met the innumerable difficulties by a policy of tolerance, disciplining itself and its surveyors to keep an open mind towards novelty. Such locutions as "experimental", "Built on peculiar principles" and "equivalent thereto" started to creep into the official vocabulary. The special notation, "Experimental (B.S.)" was introduced, with a later amendment to the effect that the word "Experimental" could be deleted after a satisfactory special survey of the vessel concerned at the end of four years. The notation (B.S.) stood for "subject to biennial survey".

This was rather a brilliant balancing act by the Society during a difficult period, a not inexpert hurdling of difficulties created at the critical moment of an almost complete change from wood to metal. It can be reckoned now that the Society's elasticity under the wise guidance of the Chairman, Thomas Chapman, evaded a crisis that might have brought the whole edifice of standardisation down in ruins. Shipbuilders, encouraged by the Society's tolerance of experiment, took to submitting their designs more readily. Perhaps the healthiest sign of all was the formation, in 1860, of the Institution of Naval Architects, which thus celebrates its Centenary as Lloyd's Register celebrates two centuries of existence.

Addressing the Institution later on, in 1863, and rather ruefully recalling the atmosphere of the uneasy years, Mr. Ritchie, one of the Society's two Principal Surveyors, observed :—

> "At the time the Committee drew up the first Rules in 1854, they felt that a classification of six, nine and twelve years, although it might approach the truth as to the probable comparative durability of the various kinds of timber of which such ships were allowed by the Rules to be built, yet these characters could not correctly indicate the durability of vessels built of metal, which only deteriorated by the wasting of the surfaces, and whose durability depended upon different laws than [sic] that of timber."

He went on:—

> "It should be borne in mind that, although the mode of constructing iron ships primarily intended by the Society's Rules is the original ordinary one of vertical frames and longitudinal plating, the Committee do not hesitate to admit into the Register Book and into the same classes, vessels otherwise constructed, if of equal strength; and they have classed ships with longitudinal frames or with diagonal frames, and many with double or cellular bottoms for water ballast."

All in all, the conciliatory policy of Lloyd's Register was paying dividends, and the atmosphere of confidence was being restored. The clinching commendation came from J. Scott Russell, builder of that wonderful, if slightly eccentric, ship, the *Great Eastern*. Speaking in public in 1860, he referred to the "*lex non scripta*, or unwritten rule of Lloyd's Register," generously admitted the Society's tolerance of experiment, and concluded that the Society "had relaxed their Rules in a way which enables them to combine with the strictness of Rules a defiance of anyone saying that they stand in the way of iron shipbuilding".

So far, so good.

CHAPTER 5   WIDENING HORIZONS

IT has been emphasised that the evolution of the modern ship cannot
be dealt with as if the long story could be broken up into so many
watertight compartments, each with a tidy chapter heading. The
wooden sailing ship did not disappear as soon as the first iron
steam-driven vessel came over the horizon, belching smoke. When
the technicians of Lloyd's Register were most onerously employed in
seeking to frame wise rules for the construction and classification of
iron ships, they were still much concerned to perfect the older rules
governing building in wood.

This was not so much because the design of the wooden ships was
always advancing in subtlety, though advances there were—notably
the recognition by naval architects of the advantage in speed conferred
by "hollow water lines": that is, roughly, the inward curve of the ship's

lines towards the bow instead of the bluff, prognathous front presented to the seas by older vessels in the "wooden walls" tradition. (The change might be graphically represented by suggesting that a sharp V was designed to cut rapidly through water in place of a bulbous U.) More than that, however, the surveyors of Lloyd's Register had to be watchful of the weights and qualities of unfamiliar new woods as the forests of the world were opened up by British shipping, and to be careful with the scantlings required by these novel materials, varying vastly in both specific gravity and powers of resistance to salt water.

This overlap between wood and iron filled the period from 1850 to 1870, roughly, with investigation proceeding on two separate fronts, so to speak. By the latter date, however, there was not much more to be learned about the construction and behaviour of the wooden sailing ship, and its fate as a carrier had indeed been sealed by the opening of the Suez Canal in 1869. Within these 20 years there nevertheless took place one of the most interesting developments in shipping history, a phase in which the old and the new in design and material were to be married and to produce children of exquisite grace.

This was the era of the Composite Ship. Vessels in this class were constructed of wooden planking over iron frames or ribs, their bottoms invariably sheathed with copper or some patent metal. The best of the composite vessels were remarkably fast. The legendary China Clippers were all of composite construction. As to the derivation of the term Clipper, authorities differ. Some hold that it was because of their capacity to cut, or clip, many days off the average sailing time between the Chinese ports and London; others that it refers to the refinement of the lines towards the ship's stern—a feature which undoubtedly added to speed but rendered the Clippers painfully liable to be "pooped" by heavy seas.

The annual Tea Race was for years regarded in Britain as a sporting event almost in the class of the Derby or the Grand National. It was a race in the sense that the first ships home from the Chinese ports with the new crop of tea earned for the merchant ransom prices in the London market; and preparations for its beginning were made as if according to a book of rules.

For days on end the fabulous Clippers would lie off the ports of

Shanghai or Foochow, waiting for the cases of tea to come down from the gardens. These arrived, loading proceeded apace but according to a special technique—the cases laid and carefully spaced on a bed of gravel, the packing between them neatly done by hand, each so precious that a few more would occasionally be tucked away in the Captain's cabin. As it usually turned out, the acknowledged leaders of the Clipper fleet got away within hours, or only a day or two, of each other; and there is some reason to believe that the more notorious skippers, each with a private wager on the side, inclined to wait for a rival's appearance just outside the starting line.

Then it was hell-for-leather half-way round the world. These composite ships were not by any means lengthy, but they carried high piles of canvas, and they were driven remorselessly by magnificent master mariners. The tale of mishaps and even total and untraceable losses was long. Meanwhile, at home, the interested merchants and brokers waited for reports from the various signal stations along the lengthy route; huge sums of money were wagered, and the odds changed from week to week as they do at the Victoria Club on the eve of the Cesarewitch.

The most wonderful ending was that of the Tea Race of 1866, when two Clippers that had left Foochow on May 30th came roaring up the English Channel at 13 knots with only an hour or so between them on September 5th, three other flyers of the day not far behind. The two in the lead were the lovely but ill-fated *Ariel*, and the *Taeping*, both products of the famous yard of Robert Steele at Greenock. Immediately behind were the *Serica*, also a Steele product, the *Fiery Cross* from a Liverpool yard, and the *Taitsing*, built by Connell at Glasgow.

Interested persons are happily able to inspect to-day one of the great Clippers, the *Cutty Sark*, restored to her original rig and general condition and preserved as a national memorial in dry dock at Greenwich. In the creation of this lovely vessel and of her great rival, the *Thermopylæ*, three men closely associated with Lloyd's Register were deeply concerned.

The *Thermopylæ*, first in the field by two years, was built by Hood of Aberdeen to the designs of Bernard Waymouth; and Waymouth was a Principal Surveyor to Lloyd's Register from 1871 until 1872 and was thereafter Secretary until 1890. The designer of the *Cutty Sark* was Hercules Linton, son of another Lloyd's Register surveyor. To complete the triangle of interest, the owner of the *Cutty Sark* was Captain John Willis, nicknamed "Old White Hat" and a member of the Committee of the Society. There is some reason to believe that the *Cutty Sark* was designed on the lines of the *Tweed*, an East Indiaman also owned by Captain Willis, and that these were in turn based on those of a captured French frigate.

It is held by some authorities that the *Cutty Sark* was a tolerably close copy of the *Thermopylæ*, though her sail area was less than that of the older ship, but it is quite certain that she was never a very lucky ship. When she was building at Dumbarton the firm of Scott & Linton ran out of funds, and the job had to be completed by the older firm of Denny Brothers. (The Scott of Scott & Linton, by the way, was a Scott Moncrieff of the family now associated with literature. He ended a long and inventive career as a successful specialist in, of all subjects! sewage disposal.) It was two years after the appearance of the *Cutty Sark* in 1870 that the two ships were matched over the long course between the Pagoda Anchorage and the Downs, and in the Tea Race of 1872 the *Cutty Sark* suffered damage of various sorts and made the passage in 119 days against the 114 of her rival. Results during later years showed that there was really very little between them, and it is tolerably certain that neither was ever such a flyer as the *Ariel* or the *Lightning*, the latter built for British owners by Mackay of Boston, Mass.

Those Clippers that were not victims of maritime disaster passed from the China tea trade to the less exacting hazards of the Australian wool trade. All had their soaring spars and elaborate rigging cut down for the sake of economy, and most of them ultimately passed into foreign hands. It is a miracle that the *Cutty Sark* survived and was recovered to display to later generations what beautiful things were created in the brilliant Indian summer of British craftsmanship in sail.

With the passing of the composite ships the Register was nearly finished with the wooden vessel. In 1864 Bernard Waymouth had been given the task of framing special Rules for the construction of composite ships. (It seems odd that, while an officer of Lloyd's Register, this gifted naval architect was allowed to accept a presumably private commission for the plans of the *Thermopylæ*.) These

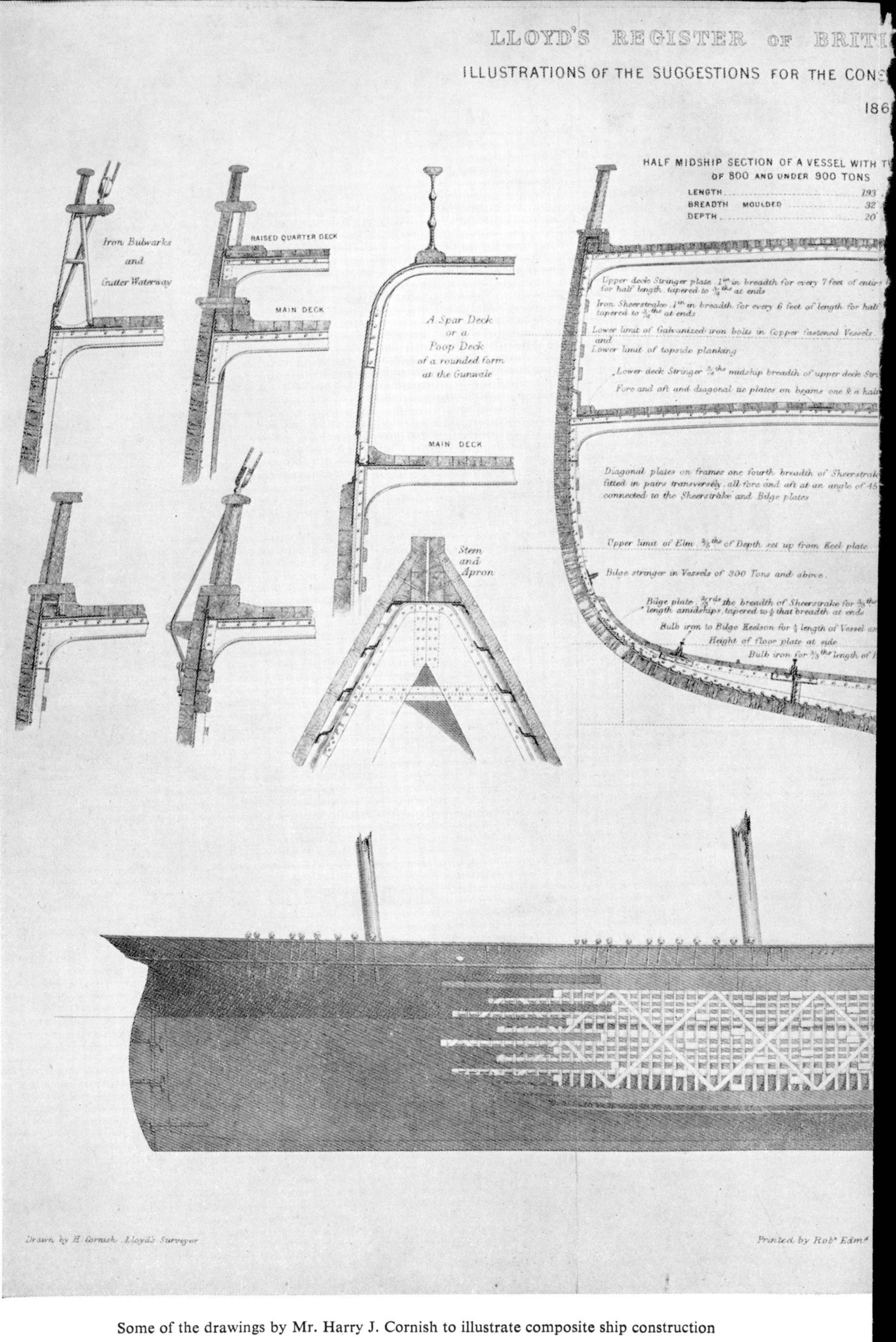

LLOYD'S REGISTER OF BRITI
ILLUSTRATIONS OF THE SUGGESTIONS FOR THE CON
186
HALF MIDSHIP SECTION OF A VESSEL WITH T
OF 800 AND UNDER 900 TONS
LENGTH 193
BREADTH MOULDED 32'
DEPTH 20'
Iron Bulwarks and Gutter Waterway
RAISED QUARTER DECK
MAIN DECK
A Spar Deck or a Poop Deck of a rounded form at the Gunwale
MAIN DECK
Stem and Apron
Upper deck Stringer plate 1in in breadth for every 7 feet of entire
for half length tapered to ¾ths at ends
Iron Sheerstrake 1in in breadth for every 6 feet of length for hal
tapered to ¾ths at ends
Lower limit of Galvanized iron bolts in Copper fastened Vessels
and
Lower limit of topside planking
Lower deck Stringer ¾ths midship breadth of upper deck Str
Fore and aft and diagonal tie plates on beams one & a hal
Diagonal plates on frames one fourth breadth of Sheerstrak
fitted in pairs transversely, all fore and aft at an angle of 45
connected to the Sheerstrake and Bilge plates
Upper limit of Elm ⅗ths of Depth set up from Keel plate
Bilge stringer in Vessels of 300 Tons and above
Bilge plate ⅔rds the breadth of Sheerstrake for ⅔ths
length amidships, tapered to ½ that breadth at ends
Bulb iron to Bilge Keelson for ½ length of Vessel an
Height of floor plate at side
Bulb iron for ⅗ths length of
Drawn by H. Cornish. Lloyd's Surveyor
Printed by Robt Edm

Some of the drawings by Mr. Harry J. Cornish to illustrate composite ship construction

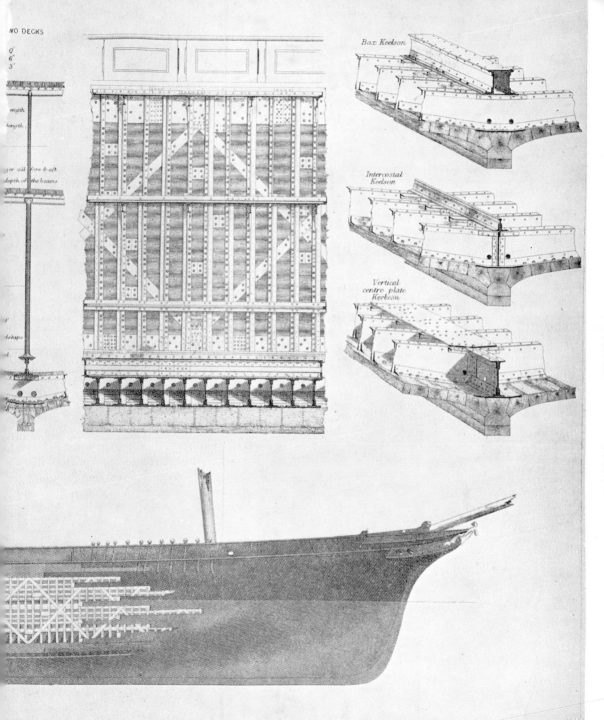

Box Keelson

Intercostal Keelson

Vertical centre plate Keelson

special Rules were concerned to some extent with the uses of different sorts of wood in any one ship, but rather more seriously with the technical question of metal fastenings within ships of this class. It had been found that the replacement of bolt-fastenings weakened by the union of conflicting materials had become a major source of expense during the overhaul of such vessels. There were also differences of opinion regarding the ideal shape of the iron frame of the composite ship, whether plain angle-iron or iron in some novel sectional form.

Waymouth's draft Rules were duly adopted, and the fact is interesting as an early case of thought and research within Lloyd's Register providing the shipbuilding industry with a constructive lead. The drawings to accompany them were the work of Harry J. Cornish, later Chief Ship Surveyor from 1900 until 1909. They were much in demand for display at international Exhibitions.

For the rest, the conventional wooden ship was not forgotten by any means, and the Rules affecting these were changed from time to time between 1850 and 1870. These alterations covered such matters as the classification of foreign-built vessels with scantlings below Lloyd's Register standards, and another set of new symbols was invented for use in the Book. As already mentioned, the use of hitherto unfamiliar woods had to be dealt with, and there was much technical concern over the "salting" of certain woods. Thus it was discovered that American oak and fir timber were greatly improved by being steeped in a solution of salt, meriting a higher character than they had been previously allowed, while certain other woods were condemned as wholly unsuitable for ship construction.

The wooden ships have almost all disappeared from the seas, and the general reader of this History need not be wearied with tables of obsolete classifications and symbols. It is right, however, to quote a gallant phrase from the first edition of the *Annals of Lloyd's Register*, 1884:—"There can be little doubt that wood ships were never better built than when they were being superseded by iron vessels".

*　　*　　*　　*　　*

As the technical officers of the Society were thus engaged in dealing with the problems created by the transition from wood to iron and

E

from sail to steam, the Committee of Lloyd's Register was called upon once more to face something like a constitutional crisis.

This had, once again, its origin in Liverpool. The essence of the movement was the unresting demand from the outports for a larger say in the management of the Society's affairs.

As we have seen, the Liverpool Register was fused with Lloyd's Register in 1845. The success of Liverpool in securing solid representation on the London Committee had aroused the envy of representative shipping men in other outports, especially in the belligerent North-East, for though some of them had been granted nominal representation on the London Committee, the condition that such delegates should be resident in London was not unnaturally resented. The outports wanted their own men on the job, whether owners, shipbuilders or underwriters; and, their feelings growing in intensity, a new campaign was opened in 1863 by a salvo from the Associations of Shipowners and Underwriters at Liverpool.

This suggested that the whole question of outport representation should be reopened, and there was little the London Committee could do but acquiesce. It was not at all that they were troubled by guilty conscience; their agreement to go into conference rested on an acknowledgement that, since the first Liverpool agreement had been made in 1845, conditions in the shipping industry had greatly changed, some ports of former importance having declined, while others had developed rapidly into prominence. In a sense, the new climate of political opinion, so to call it, marched with the change from wood and sail to iron and steam.

The upshot of the 1863 negotiations was an agreement that ten new members should be added to the existing Committee in London. With characteristic vigour the Liverpool delegates gained the point that four of these should be nominated from Merseyside: two to be elected by the Liverpool Shipowners' Association, two by the Liverpool Underwriters' Association. For the rest, there were to be two members from the Clyde, one underwriter and one shipowner; one merchant from Tyneside; one shipowner from the Wear; one merchant from Hull and one merchant from Bristol. A year later the Committee was still further increased by one other member—an underwriter from the Tees and Hartlepool district.

This was a considerable move towards the proper enfranchisement of the outports and a better balance of national opinion within the Society. Even so, the aggressive Liverpudlians took up their cudgels again in 1871 and secured still larger representation on the Committee; with the almost automatic result that the other outports took to pressing their special cases with still greater urgency.

The end of this long tale of provincial revolt came in 1883 with a complete readjustment of outport representation. After long and full deliberation it was decided that the number of Committee members should be raised from 41 to 50, taking into account the claims of ports to the positions of consequence they had reached during the years of rapid Victorian expansion. This arrangement gave Glasgow and the Tyne two additional members, the Tees and Sunderland one each. New members were appointed for the district of Cardiff, Newport and Swansea, for the district of Leith, Dundee and Aberdeen, and for the port of Greenock.

The reconstitution was to serve for many years to come. The Society could now be held to provide a truly national Register of Shipping. During the five years before the agreement was reached, Lloyd's Register had surveyed and classed 90 per cent of the merchant vessels built in the United Kingdom.

*　　*　　*　　*　　*

The phase of development thus satisfactorily ended had embraced an important extension of the Society's activity, the first move towards international status. This was the appointment of surveyors to represent and act for Lloyd's Register overseas.

The impulse in this direction came from that inveterate "pressure group," the shipping community of Liverpool, and was indeed one of the motives that had inspired its original revolt against the Society. It illustrates an extremely interesting aspect of the mercantile history of Britain and what subsequently became the Commonwealth.

The early settlers in North America, especially Canada, had included a considerable number of emigrants, many from Cornwall, who were reasonably skilled in the crafts of wooden shipbuilding. About their new-found homes on the American coasts were abundant supplies of native wood, mostly fir and oak, though these were hardly up to European standards in quality. Many of those early settlers thus settled down to give their new life a variegated rhythm—clearing the virgin woods and cultivating the fresh soil during the warm months and, in the winter, building wooden sailing ships.

These were mostly rather small, most of them rigged no more elaborately than as schooners or brigs. They were rather coarse jobs by the standards of Lloyd's Register, even if they made up for lack of finesse of design and craftsmanship with unusually heavy scantlings. For many years the Society declined to classify ships built in North America, except in the odd case, and this became a serious grievance in Liverpool, the leading port of the North American trade. In the normal run of things, this trade was a simple exchange of British coal outwards for Canadian timber inwards. When, however, the incomers were well settled along the shores of the river and gulf of St. Lawrence, they entered the business on their own account, sending cargoes of timber to Britain in their own new-built ships, the latter to be sold in the old country as opportunity occurred. Thus in Liverpool and Leith particularly British shipowners acquired considerable fleets of Canadian-built vessels, and it galled them that these were refused classification by Lloyd's Register.

The separate Liverpool Register founded in 1835 was partly inspired by the local desire to give vessels in this class some sort of status in classification, and the issue remained a point of difference between the Society and Liverpool, even after the compromise of 1845. As it turned out, the first move towards breaking the deadlock came direct from Canada.

This was made in a letter addressed to the Secretary of Lloyd's Register from St. John, New Brunswick, proposing on the authority of a number of solid shipowners in that port that the Society appoint a surveyor there, these men of business guaranteeing a salary of £300 for the period of five years. A similar suggestion was soon afterwards received from Quebec.

No doubt these proposals shook some of the more conservative parties in London, many of them old enough to remember Trafalgar and the glorious days of the East Indiamen, but a shrewder majority perceived that the Society's writ must eventually be extended across the seas, and that English-speaking North America was one of the likeliest fields of shipbuilding expansion. In 1852, therefore, Captain Menzies of Leith, himself an experienced shipbuilder, was appointed Exclusive Surveyor for Quebec and the River St. Lawrence.

This appointment immediately proved successful, and only a year later another exclusive surveyorship was established at St. John, New Brunswick, whence the original suggestion had come, with two assistant surveyors allocated to Prince Edward Island and Mira-michi respectively. Within a few years six experienced surveyors were working in Canada for Lloyd's Register, and the consequent improvement in design and workmanship was remarkable. These overseas officers of the Society did more than conduct the normal inspections at three stages of each building process as laid down in the Rules; they had the building of every vessel under constant supervision. This led Captain Menzies to suggest to London that every ship so produced should have on its certificate from Lloyd's Register the phrase "Built under Special Survey".

This suggestion was adopted and the results gave great satisfaction to Canadian producers and British purchasers alike. Indeed, the Society went out of its way to award a special symbol in the Register Book for all vessels built in terms of this special survey, the familiar ✠ symbol. It stands to this day as denoting that a ship so classified has been built under the supervision of the surveyors in accordance with the Society's Rules and Regulations.

There will be much to say later on about the expansion of the Society's scope and authority in foreign parts, but it is fitting to note at this point how the foundations of a vast international service were laid during the sixth, seventh and eighth decades of the 19th Century, and that the impulse came out of the Canadian experiment.

In 1856 a Mr. Pretious, a shipwright surveyor from the staff on the Tyne, went to Rotterdam as Surveyor for Holland and Belgium, only to be recalled after three years for lack of work on a reasonably profitable scale, and it was not until 1866 that Mr. L. Meyer was appointed a non-exclusive surveyor for the same region but with headquarters at Antwerp this time. This appointment proved sufficiently successful to persuade Dutch and Belgian shipping men to ask for more and the Society to post deputies to Amsterdam, Rotterdam and Veendam.

Such were the beginnings of a vast extension of the Society's influence. In 1869 surveyors were appointed to a wide range of ports between Bordeaux and Shanghai; and three years later the scope was extended to include centres from Bergen, Norway, to Hobart, Tasmania. In all, during the Seventies the number of non-exclusive surveyors abroad rose from five to more than 60.

The fact demonstrates at once the rapid development of the shipping industry in that period of expansion and the new resilience of the Society. It is of much historical interest that the transfer of Mr. J. Tucker from Quebec to Shanghai in 1870 was indirectly due to redundancy in Canada, where the building of ships in wood was by that time in rapid decline. Once more, the history of Lloyd's Register faithfully mirrors the trends in world shipbuilding over a long period of time. It will be shown in due course that, what with wars, political changes and economic vicissitudes, the pattern is almost always continually changing—but with the Society always alert to meet the changes in its capacity as an international authority of impregnable integrity.

*　　*　　*　　*　　*

With so much solid work done after a few false starts and recurrent crises, the Society was justified in organising with confidence the formal recognition of its own 50th anniversary: that is, dating from the reorganisation of 1834. This was contrived at a dinner in the Cannon Street Hotel on October 30th, 1884. The reports indicate that the occasion was a weighty one, the toast list lengthy and the speeches far from brief. One hardly expects memorable utterances to be made on such occasions, and this gathering was shadowed by the clouds of a transient depression in trade. As to that, Sir James Laing of Sunderland was able to declare sensibly:—

> "The nation has had a glorious past, and although it is now severely depressed, its energy is unimpaired, and I have every faith in the hopefulness of the future.
> "I can remember how in 1840 there was a state of things tenfold worse than anything now experienced. At that time in the East India Docks, ships were lying side by side, tier by tier, in a state of idleness, and with little likelihood of employment. In the city they were known as the 'Rotten Row'!
> "But this had an end, as the existing depression will have an end, and I am convinced there is a great future before us."

Finally, speaking with the downright voice of Liverpool, Sir

Thomas B. Royden put into a few cogent words the real meaning of the celebration:—

> "I venture to say that wherever a British ship goes, bearing the classification of Lloyd's Register, in whatever part of the world, she is accepted as being fit to carry any cargo offered."

The Chairman at this dinner was Mr. W. H. Tindall who had become Chairman of the Society three years before, but it is not disrespectful to the memory of a gentleman who held that high office until 1899 to suggest it was a pity that Thomas Chapman had not survived to be in the seat of honour.

Thomas Chapman, afterwards a Fellow of the Royal Society, had been elected Chairman of Lloyd's Register in 1835, immediately after the fusion of the Red and Green Books. It will be recalled that, during one period of stringency, he had personally guaranteed the salaries of the officers, and he had steered the affairs of Lloyd's Register among the shoals of crisis and round the rocks of obduracy with wisdom, pliability and firmness. He was the true Father of Lloyd's Register as we know it in its unique position to-day, and as such he was a national servant of infinitely more importance than many whose names are hammered into the minds of school children.

Just a few facts and figures suggest the magnitude of the work done under his presidency. Subscribers to Lloyd's Register increased in number from 721 in 1834 to nearly 3,500 in 1884. Four influential Marine Insurance corporations had supported the Society in 1834; the number had risen to 21 fifty years later. The largest vessel classed in the 1834 Book was the wood ship *George the Fourth* of 1,438 tons, while pride of place in 1884 was held by the *City of Rome*, an iron steamer of 8,144 tons . . . and may the present writer be allowed the luxury of recalling how, as a small boy on the shores of the Firth of Clyde, he used to watch the comings and goings of that lovely vessel on her last voyages? She was built at Barrow-in-Furness for the Inman Line and passed to the Anchor Line for their Clyde–New York trade. With her fiddle bow, three funnels and four masts rigged fore-and-aft, she had the grace of a yacht . . . The 1834 Book measured $8 \times 5 \times 1\frac{1}{2}$ inches and weighed $1\frac{3}{4}$ lbs., but it required a tome of $10\frac{1}{4} \times 8\frac{1}{2} \times 3$ inches and weighing 7 lbs. to contain the information available in the year of the 50th Birthday celebrations.

CHAPTER 6   LOAD LINES AND IRON SHIPS

B EFORE it could face the 50th anniversary celebration with reasonable self-satisfaction Lloyd's Register had had to adapt itself to a
number of technical changes in shipbuilding processes during a
period of rapid expansion. The gradual transition from wood to iron
as the chief element in construction was always the dominant
concern, but the 19th Century produced certain crises in which,
oddly enough, public and political interests were as much involved as
those of the pure technicians.

None of these remains a relevant issue in 1960; the old fires of
controversy have burned out long ago, and the matters of material
concern have been swept into the limbo of the merely antique by
the unceasing tides of progress. These small crises were nevertheless
critical moments in the evolution of British shipping, and they

excellently illustrate how the Society—as, in the American term, a Bureau of Standards with increasing esteem and ever-growing responsibility—was called upon to adjust itself to novelties in invention, methods, use of materials and so on.

It will be recalled that the early Register Books gave marks for soundness of equipment as well as for the excellence of any ship's construction, but even after the reconstitution of 1834 the Rules merely specified the number of anchors and the length of chain cable required for vessels of different sizes and made no mention of dimensions or tests. It was that lively man, Thomas Chapman, who first suggested to his colleagues that ships' cables should be tested and certified, but the notion was not taken up, and the Society's approach to the problem was only tentative over a period of years. In 1853, however, the Committee came round to laying it down that cables should be tested before a vessel might be classed, and in due course the experts produced a table shewing the number and weight of anchors, and the length and size of cables, hawsers and warps appropriate to various sizes and types of ship. Favourable allowance was to be made for chain cables that could withstand on public proving-machines the tests laid down by the Admiralty.

In 1860, however, the whole question of the equipment of merchant vessels came up in the House of Commons. This was the somewhat unexpected result of public agitation: in fact, a strange instance of popular pressure bearing on an essentially technical question.

The agitation was inspired in part by the proud romanticism of the British attitude to ships and seamen, even if most members of the public could not be trusted to distinguish as between a cable and a capstan. The other force sprang from popular prejudice against the ironmasters of South Staffordshire and East Worcestershire, the main centres of the chainmaking industry. The record of these manufacturers as employers of labour was not at all good, and the chainmaking towns were breeding-grounds of Radical discontent. Under such pressures, at all events, Parliament set up a Select Committee to inquire into the manufacture of chains and cables.

It was not until 1864 that the findings of this body were incorporated in an Act for "Regulating the Proving and Sale of Chain Cables and Anchors". This provided for the licensing of Public Proving Houses under the jurisdiction of the Board of Trade, and the effect of the regulation must have surprised its promoters. Warned by legislation of the necessity to take concerted action towards providing approved testing facilities near their works, the ironmasters combined to float joint stock companies to finance them. Proving Houses were opened at Tipton and Netherton in 1865 to begin with. Then it dawned on some watchful and suspicious persons that the manufacturer could without great difficulty obtain a licence for a testing machine and proceed to issue certificates guaranteeing the soundness of his own goods! Whatever the basis of these suspicions, an amendment of 1871 to the Act of 1864 laid it down that licences to test cables should be granted by the Board of Trade only to certain corporations or public bodies.

Lloyd's Register had in fact anticipated even the 1864 Act. In 1862 the Committee ruled that all anchors and chain cables for vessels to be classed in the Register Book must be tested and certified at a public weighing machine; and the Society went to the considerable expense of setting up a Proving House at Poplar. Only a year later the Committee was insisting that no testing would be recognised unless done at an establishment belonging to a disinterested corporation and open to an inspector appointed by Lloyd's Register—surely a bold and self-confident anticipation of what Parliament would lay down in the following year.

When the Act was amended in 1871 the strength of the Society's position was fully recognised. It was found that the testing certificates issued by some of the joint stock companies owning Proving Houses were unacceptable, and the Board of Trade itself approached the Society with the handsome statement that "they could look to no other beyond the Committee of Lloyd's Register to ensure an impartial test". The Committee agreed to accept this responsibility and accepted licences for these private Proving Houses. A General Superintendent of Proving Houses was appointed by the Society, and local superintendents worked under him. The Proving House at Poplar was disposed of to Trinity House in 1873, and Lloyd's Register became for practical purposes, under the Board of Trade, the ultimate authority on the fitness of anchors and iron cables.

This success ended a short but interesting phase of British industrial history, and almost immediately the Society became deeply involved in another aspect of safety at sea, and another in which popular feeling was engaged. This was the agitation, usually associated with the name of Samuel Plimsoll, for the definition and legal establishment of a safe load line—that is, of a level duly marked on her sides, beyond which a ship could not be loaded with safety in sea-going conditions.

Samuel Plimsoll need not be grudged his posthumous fame as the originator of "the Plimsoll Line". He was born at Bristol in 1824 and no doubt acquired as a birthright a considerable knowledge of general shipping conditions. After a spell in a Sheffield brewery, he set up for himself in the coal trade in London and, prospering, took up with passion the cause of seamen exploited in unseaworthy craft: a study that provided him with material for "Our Seamen", published in 1873.

Plimsoll was giving popular expression to the exposure of real abuses. Too many unscrupulous parties of that period were buying up rotten ships, insuring them heavily and then sending them to sea, and that without much hope of safe return. These were the "coffin ships" of popular legend, and Plimsoll hammered the theme loud and long. He got himself elected Member of Parliament for Derby in 1868, and it was largely his doing that the Merchant Shipping Act of 1876 defined proper methods of dealing with different types of cargo and laid it down that a ship must bear on her sides the mark shewing the maximum depth to which she might be loaded in salt water.

It may be observed that the underwriters naturally took a profound interest in the establishment of a proper load line; and, unfortunately for the romantics, Lloyd's Register had seriously addressed itself to the subject when Samuel Plimsoll was still a ten-year-old boy in Bristol. In 1835 the Committee had worked out and propounded what came to be known as Lloyd's Rule—that a merchant vessel should have a freeboard of three inches for every foot in depth of her hold. This was a rough and ready measurement to be sure, but it was at least a beginning, and it served for many years. And then, in 1870, six years before the passing of the Merchant Shipping Act for which Plimsoll had so briskly agitated, the Society acted with such decision in the load line business that it found itself involved in litigation.

This arose out of a wholly technical point. At that period ship-owners exploiting suitable routes over warm seas were putting into service passenger vessels with what came to be called awning decks.

These were built up above the main deck, and while the total weight of material involved might not be great, that little weight, *plus* the extra height above water level, could have a bearing on any ship's classification with the Society. The Society's Rules insisted that, in such cases, there should be scuppers through the sides of awning 'tween decks and sizeable ports on the main deck below, to allow for the free escape of water shipped in a seaway. It came to the knowledge of the Committee, however, that some shipowners, so that their vessels might be laden more heavily, were permanently closing the scuppers and ports on the main deck level; and firm action was taken in 1873. The Society in that year withdrew the privilege of classification from all ships of the awning-deck type that had had their main deck scuppers permanently closed.

Furthermore—and still in anticipation of the Act of 1876—it was ordained by the Rules that, if main deck scuppers were to be permanently closed in new vessels of the type, then that vessel must be marked with a load line approved by the Society's Surveyors— that is, if classification was sought. And since abuses of the Rule continued, in 1875 the Society determined that no awning-deck vessel could be classified that did not carry the clear mark of the Society's approval, the ordinance to be retrospective. For this purpose there was devised an unmistakable symbol, thus ᴸ◆ᴿ.

Now, this was a bold step. It seemed to assert what Lloyd's Register of Shipping had never possessed: the right to enforce those standards it believes to be desirable; and it was challenged. An important shipping company, owning several ships of the awning-deck type, declined to comply with the Committee's requirements. The characters of their vessels were therefore expunged from the Register Book. The shipowners retorted by raising a test-action, claiming damages to the tune of £1,000.

Their action did not succeed, the Judge observing:—

> "The Pursuers' case depends on the validity of their proposition, that the facts averred by them imply a contract between them and the Defenders with respect to the . . . whereby the classification of that vessel on the Register shall be preserved so long as the Rules and Regulations of the Association in force at the date of the original registration in 1872 are complied with. I cannot sustain this proposition."

And he added:—

> "It would be a grave misfortune, and greatly impair public confidence in the Association (Lloyd's Register), if a Court of Law were to hold that they were under implied contract with respect to all ships already classified which compelled them to continue the classification after they had become satisfied that it was undeserved, and therefore misleading."

The shipowners appealed against this decision and lost, and the position of the Society was thus immensely strengthened. It established the right of the Committee to alter the Rules as experience may show to be necessary and to apply such alterations retrospectively.

Lloyd's Register were next engaged in some controversy over the question of suitable freeboards for ships of the spar-deck type, a design favoured by owners of passenger vessels, but the vogue of the spar-deck ship was short-lived, and the affair merits only this bald mention as an example of the Society's involvement in every phase of shipbuilding. It was to be much more seriously involved when Plimsoll's campaign got into its stride and he had, through Parliament, secured for the Board of Trade powers to detain overladen ships as unseaworthy.

The mere statement begs a large question—at what point is a ship overladen? The question is largely empirical. At all events, faced with its new task, the Board of Trade, as was now becoming its habit, asked for the co-operation of Lloyd's Register and the help of its surveyors in detecting suspect vessels at the various ports.

This was asking a good deal, and almost imposing on the Society a quasi-judicial responsibility, but Thomas Chapman replied as Chairman that the Committee must always be interested in the preservation of life and property at sea, and that the surveyors' services would be gladly placed at the disposal of the Government. That point conceded, the Board of Trade went on to ask the Society for assistance in laying down at least the first principles of a scheme for determining the proper load draught of water for merchant vessels, and it was agreed that representatives of Lloyd's Register should join with nominees of the Board of Trade and of the Liverpool Underwriters' Register in a Committee to examine the problem.

This Committee did not last long. Bluntly, the problem was too big for it. It was a problem for experts, and to experts it duly returned;

in fact, to the skilled surveying staff of Lloyd's Register. Nor was this fresh attack on the problem inspired by the Board of Trade. It arose out of the Committee's firm desire to grapple with and master a question of devilish intricacy. To that end the by now elaborate machinery of Lloyd's Register was thrown into forward gear. Surveyors were instructed to take note of the depths of immersion of ships at the various ports. Many of the principal shipowning firms agreed to provide particulars of their practice. The vast amount of material thus collected was put into the hands of the Society's Chief Surveyor, Benjamin Martell, with instructions to frame tables of freeboard suitable for every type of vessel.

Martell was one of the Society's most distinguished servants. He had succeeded Bernard Waymouth as Chief Surveyor in 1872 and remained in that key post until 1900. As early as 1873 he had been engaged in the study of this intricate subject and had provided a set of tables for the benefit of a Royal Commission on Unseaworthy Ships. These had been accepted, but the material provided by the new investigation called for a new approach to the subject, and it was not until January, 1882, that Mr. Martell was able to present his revised conclusions.

The layman sufficiently interested in the technique of the load line can quite easily find material for study in any good encyclopædia, and it is sufficient here to say that Martell's rules for different types of ships were accepted by the Committee and passed on to shipowners, shipbuilders and other competent persons for comment. The observations thus evoked led to further analysis and modification of the Tables, and they were published in August, 1882. The Board of Trade issued in 1886 its own Freeboard Tables as recommended by a Committee with the following significant admission:—

> "The Tables submitted herewith are of the same general form as those hitherto adopted by Lloyd's Register Office, and like them involve the reservation above water of a regulated minimum percentage of total buoyancy. At the same time these tables secure a sufficient height of deck above water to which the Board of Trade advisers have justly attached much importance . . . The Tables as now submitted involve only such limited modifications of the freeboards assigned by the latest Tables of Lloyd's Register Office, as Mr. Benjamin Martell is able to freely accept and cordially concur with."

Allowing for the magnificently split infinitive in the last sentence, this was a handsome acknowledgment of the soundness and brilliance of the work done by Benjamin Martell with the encouragement of the Committee of Lloyd's Register. The Board of Trade, in fact, accepted as valid all freeboard certificates issued by Lloyd's Register and thus conferred on the Society once more all but executive authority in a shipbuilding matter of prime importance and international range. For a long time thereafter the Society's officers were kept busy assigning freeboards in response to the requests that poured in from every port in the country at the rate of at least 700 a year for ten years on end. It will be seen later on, however, that the creation of this near-monopoly in the matter of the load line was to provoke a breakaway movement of first-class importance.

The strength of iron cables and the buoyancy of ships are no longer such controversial issues, but it is right that this History should take considerable account of these proceedings of last century. The Society's successes in tackling two major problems and setting up standards universally acceptable were very important factors in establishing its unique authority as a wholly detached and utterly dependable buttress of the highest technical standards.

*　　*　　*　　*　　*

While the Society and its technical advisers were thus engaged, they were still grappling all the time with the obdurate problem of how to arrive at a fool-proof and generally acceptable formula for the classification of iron ships.

This, as we have noted, had been left in 1857 in a state of somewhat uneasy balance as between the Society's natural fondness for strict rules and the novelties continually being introduced by progressive shipbuilders. Conscious of imperfection within the scheme, the Committee therefore instructed every member of the surveying staff to make recommendations for revision, and at the same time it took the advice of the principal iron shipbuilders throughout the country. These inquiries produced a satisfactory degree of unanimity, and in 1863 a set of revised rules was published.

These were based on the general agreement that the former practice of classifying iron vessels for given terms of years was not appropriate to the tough nature of the material. In other words, the real character of an iron ship was to be determined by the thickness of the metal that had gone into her construction, and so long as the original scantlings were properly maintained, it was unreasonable that she should be down-graded on the score of years alone. The Committee therefore determined to class iron ships in three grades; and one fancies that the appropriate officials must have had some fun in devising the appropriate symbols.

These were Ⓐ1, Ⓐ1, and Ⓐ1, the allotted class to be retained so long as the vessels were maintained in a state of efficiency. Classes Ⓐ1 and Ⓐ1 applied to ships that had been built in accordance with the Rules or with equal regard for good workmanship; the Ⓐ1 symbol applied to ships which, meriting the general A1 character, had not been built according to the Rules. Periodical surveys were to be made on a system rather less rigorous than had previously been enforced. A new approach to tolerance in the Society's attitude towards the iron ship was a certain relaxation of the old rules regarding the weight of scantlings, originally laid down on the basis of experience with wood ships. It was now allowed that these could safely be reduced, especially towards the bows and sterns of iron vessels.

But that was still not the end of a controversial matter. The redoubtable Bernard Waymouth had been bending his considerable intellectual powers to what was for him no doubt a fascinating problem, and he came out in 1870 with some revolutionary thoughts on the subject.

Again the issue was technical in the extreme, but Waymouth's conclusion was, roughly, that the old system of fixing the scantlings for iron ships in terms of the under-deck tonnage was mistaken. For one thing, the tonnage could not be determined until the vessel had been completed, and Waymouth concluded that the scantlings of iron vessels should be determined only in relation to their dimensions.

One does not require to be a trained naval architect to perceive that this shift of emphasis was revolutionary; and the suggestion was poorly received by some of Mr. Waymouth's colleagues. An interesting situation was created, wherein the two Principal Surveyors, James Martin and J. Horatio Ritchie, strongly favoured the older method and advised the Committee in that sense. In the deliberations that ensued Benjamin Martell, of whom we have already learned something much to his credit, fought tooth and nail for the Waymouth plan. His enthusiasm was sufficient to convince the General Committee that Waymouth was in the rights of the matter, and the new Rules were adopted.

Is it significant that Bernard Waymouth became a Principal Surveyor in 1871, that Martin and Ritchie vacated their posts as Joint Principal Surveyors shortly afterwards, and that Benjamin Martell succeeded Waymouth in 1872 as—the title having been changed—Chief Surveyor?

The Waymouth Rules involved the contrivance of still another set of symbols, but this was nearly the last of a long series and one which, with modifications, is in use to the present day. It was now laid down that iron ships should be classified as 100A1, 90A1, 80A1 and so on, these assignations to be retained so long as the vessels concerned passed special surveys at regular intervals. There thus emerged at length the designation that is the prime mark of a ship's fitness to this day, ⊹100A1.

One of the last stages in the evolution of iron ship classification was reached in 1885, when Lloyd's Register was still growing mightily in stature and the reorganised Society had triumphantly celebrated its 50th birthday.

The old feeling of rebellion in Liverpool against the preference shown in the Society's Rules for home-built ships over those built in British North America had never entirely faded; and later fresh criticism arose about the method of classing iron ships for limited terms of years. So in 1862 a new Liverpool Register was established, the Underwriters' Registry for Iron Vessels.

This Register lasted with reasonable success until 1885, but it had long been recognised on both sides that, the standards and prestige of Lloyd's Register continually improving, the simultaneous existence of a separate Register of iron ships was a wasteful duplication. The parties therefore came together with the approval of the respective Chairmen, Mr. W. H. Tindall of Lloyd's Register and Mr. Alfred Holt of the Liverpool Registry, and it was not long before agreement was reached whereby the organisation on Merseyside ceased to function. The Liverpool Register had had its own symbols of classification—A⁂1, A✳1, A1 and A—and it was agreed that these should continue to be used in Lloyd's book. Therein these characters appeared for many years until time swallowed up the survivors of the fusion.

The Liverpool Register had contained the names of 1,066 vessels, 365 of these classified in Lloyd's Register. The amalgamation brought the total of ships accounted for in the Society's Book up to 9,100 and more.

It may be added that the peace treaty with Liverpool in 1885 did not finally subdue the schismatic inclinations of the turbulent outports.

*   *   *   *   *

It is one of the most agreeable features of the history of Lloyd's Register during the second half of the 19th Century that the Society, much taken up with controversy about the load line and such issues, involved in always anxious negotiation with the proud men of Liverpool, found time to establish a separate Register of Yachts.

Many readers, concerned with the fitness of the British Merchant Navy, may regard this departure as bordering on the frivolous, but it was not so. Under steady Royal patronage, yachting had been for a long time a special and elegant expression of the British genius in seafaring. The craft of yacht design and building had become an exquisite specialty, and many a valuable principle of importance in the construction of larger craft was proved in the small racing boats of the inshore waters.

As industrial wealth increased, indeed, yachts grew big, capable of ocean voyaging: the vogue culminating in those lovely flowers of the steam shipbuilding art, such great steam yachts as Lipton's *Erin*, Goelet's *Nahma*, Lord Brassey's *Sunbeam*, Lady Yule's *Nahlin* and the rest. Since one of these fiddle-bowed queens would carry more than 50 souls in passengers and crew on an extended voyage, perhaps across the Atlantic, the safety factor was fully as important as in the case of the average merchant vessel.

No doubt the impetus towards the creation of a Register of Yachts came out of the fact that the sport was naturally much in favour among men who had done well in one branch or another of the shipping industry. The first move came in fact from within the yachting fraternity. This was in 1877, when Mr. Dixon Kemp set about organising a movement among some of the leading Yacht Clubs. These pioneers had apparently dreamed of setting up an organisation of their own, but it soon dawned on them that it would be merely sensible to use, if they could secure them, the existing services of Lloyd's Register and its skilled staff. To this the Committee of the Society agreed.

So the first issue of Lloyd's Register of Yachts appeared in 1878. It contained particulars of as many yachts as the compilers could lay hands on, but it did not deal with classification. There were 320 subscribers to this first edition; that total had risen to nearly 1,000 in 1884. This later edition included as much information as was available about yachts owned abroad, and it contained a list of British and Foreign Yacht Clubs with their flags and burgees on coloured plates.

Yachting enjoyed its most splendid period between the 1880's and 1914. In 1902 the Society was persuaded to compile a separate Register of American and Canadian yachts, and this has proved a popular and successful work of reference since its first appearance in May, 1903—allowing, that is, for breaks occasioned by two World Wars.

It is an equally interesting fact that the classification of yachts and their survey under construction became quite a substantial part of the Society's business. During the first seven years of the Yacht Register's existence more than 600 yachts were submitted for survey with a view to classification. Rules were framed to cover the construction and periodical examination of yachts, whether of wood, iron or composite construction; and when the Society issued its first Rules for steel ships in 1888, separate Rules for yachts built of that material—mostly large sailing craft and elegant steam yachts of the period—were also published.

Conditions in yachting have vastly changed since the spacious 1880's. Various factors, mainly that of economics, have favoured a vogue of quite small yachts for both cruising and racing, but it is a fact that the increasingly noisy conditions of modern living have driven more and more people to find pleasure in this form of recreation. There will be more to say later on about the expansion and specialised workings of this picturesque branch of the Society's activities.

CHAPTER 7   THE ADVANCE CONTINUES

IT was not until 1874 that the Society appointed its first engineer
surveyor. He was William Parker, one of 87 candidates for the
job, and he held his post with distinction, first as Principal, then
Chief, Engineer Surveyor until his term of service ended in 1890. Two
junior engineer surveyors were appointed at the same time, one at
Liverpool and the other for the Clyde, and two further appointments
were made only a few months later.

To-day when engineering in its innumerable branches forms so
large a part of the work of Lloyd's Register, we may wonder that this
step was taken so late in the day. It is merely amusing that one hopeful
spirit, otherwise unknown to fame, applied for an engineering
appointment as far back as 1838 and had his suggestion politely
declined. Rather more significant is the fact that a serious suggestion,

its origin unknown, was made to the Committee in 1865, that ships' machinery should be surveyed during construction, but this was turned down, the Board of Trade indicating that it did not insist on this sort of inspection. Contemporary thinking, in short, continued to be taken up mainly with the quality of hulls.

The wise men of the Committee of Lloyd's Register could not have been blind to the rapid development of the steam engine as applied to ship propulsion. The primitive side lever engine, with power supplied from a rather dangerous boiler at a pressure of about 3½ lb. per square inch—most of that had disappeared by the 1840's. The screw propeller, vastly improved engines of the steeple, oscillating and other types had come into use along with gearing between the low speed engines and higher speed propellers. The important, almost revolutionary, application of the principle of surface condensation came in the 1860's along with "compounding", the use of steam expansively in two stages in coupled cylinders. Triple expansion, demanding boiler pressures up to 60 lb. per square inch and therefore boilers of novel design—so much of this the work of an engineering genius, John Elder of Govan—was in use before the Society appointed its first engineer surveyor.

The shipbuilding-engineering industry, concentrated along the banks of just a few northern rivers, was developing at breakneck speed indeed—rather faster, one can see nowadays, than either the Board of Trade or the Society quite realised or would admit. It was really a subtly fascinating conflict between mechanical progress and stout English tradition. It is necessary, however, to see the issue in proportion. The Society had been deeply rooted in the tradition of sail and the sanctity of any vessel's hull; and it was after all not a huge desert in time that separated, say, Robert Napier's first four Cunarders in 1840 from the first compounded ships, *Inca* and *Valparaiso*, that started trading between Liverpool and South American ports in 1856.

Within the inherited tradition, therefore, the Society had not felt imperatively obliged to be vastly interested in the development of machinery. The Rules issued in 1834 had dealt with the then special case of vessels "navigated by Steam", but as for the state of boilers and machinery at the twice-yearly survey, that was to be certified by "some competent *Master Engineer*"—a not notably reassuring term.

If the requisite certificate was forthcoming, the notation MC (Machinery Certified) went with the vessel's other particulars in the Register Book, but if it did not, her hull classification did not suffer. In other words, classification of hull and engines was not inter-dependent as it is to-day.

A move of some importance was made in 1869, however. In that year the Committee laid down for the future the stipulation that engines and boilers would be considered as part of a vessel's equip-ment and, if that was found to be unsatisfactory, the figure 1 of the cherished A1 designation would be withheld. But the general attitude of the Society at that period is amusingly reflected in the fact that, when the need for engine surveys was recognised, the Com-mittee still felt that the job was within the capabilities of the existing ship surveying staff—a suggestion these experts were quick to discourage.

So the engineer surveyors appointed in 1874 embarked on a task that was novel and no doubt delicate in face of the old emphasis on the importance of hulls alone. It has been shown that the Society had been concerned with the issue of safety where mechanical devices were concerned, in respect of boilers, anchors and cables, for example. As it chanced, the new engineer department was directed at once to turn its attention to another problem affecting safety. This was the arrangement of sea cocks, inlet and outlet valves, and pipes in steam-driven vessels, and it was a much more important concern than would appear at first sight.

Any one who has travelled in a big ship or just seen one in dock must have marvelled at the number of its orifices and pondered the complexity of its inward parts. In the early steamships the arrange-ment of these ducts had hardly been systematised, and the very fervour of the early experimental engineers and the pragmatical application of their own glad discoveries had made of almost every ship of the period a Chinese puzzle of cocks and gadgets that the carelessness of an engineer or even a fireman could turn into a fatal source of leakage.

The recommendations of the Society's engineer surveyors in such matters were welcome to shipowners in particular, and order was gradually restored. The experience of the pioneers in the more advanced shipyards throughout the country soon put the Committee

Certificate for Vessels Navigated by Steam.

_____ *Day of* _____ , 1834.
_____ certify that the whole of the Boilers and Machinery of the
Steam Vessel _____ belonging to _____ whereof
_____ is Master, 113 Tons, have been carefully inspected and
examined by _____ at _____ , and that _____ find the same to be at
this time in good order and safe working condition.
Witness _____

_____ **Master Engineer.**

The following is a true Account of the Particulars of the Machinery of the Steam Vessel above named:

Engines.		Boilers.	
Nº.		Whether iron or copper	
Estimated Power		Working pressure	
Diameter of Paddle-wheels		If it can be increased at pleasure	
Length of Paddles		If any and what means of changing the water	
Breadth of Paddles		without extinguishing the fires and	
If upon the first or second motion		blowing off	
Nº. of revolutions per minute			
Size and condition of the holding down bolts			
		Nº. of feed pumps	
		How attached	
		State of the boilers	
Fuel.			
Where stowed			
If in contact with boiler		What clear space upon the topside of the boiler	
For what quantity room is provided		Dº. at the end	
If liable to get wetted		Dº. round the chimney	
		Pumps.	
		Nº. of hand pumps	
		If any attached to engine, their purpose and power	
		Nº. of force pumps, with a branch and hose of sufficient length to reach to every part of the vessel	

_____ Master Engineer.

A Master Engineer's certificate issued in December,
1834, for the machinery of the *Sir Francis Drake*

in possession of a vast amount of material regarding marine engineering practice, and the formulation of rules followed quickly. Safety was still the predominant factor. The concern was with the strength of boilers and the propriety of the scantlings for boilers and machinery. There was no attempt to impose restrictions on the design and proportion of engines.

Confidence in the work of the engineer surveyors was established with quite remarkable rapidity. Machinery surveys in those early days were not nearly so close as they are now, but again the ship-owners in particular valued the work being done by a relatively small staff, and many of the leading lines asked for special attention to be paid to the machinery installed in their vessels; some even offered to pay special fees for the service. To this the Committee agreed. The engineering staff was increased, and soon the system of special survey that had so long applied to hulls was applied to machinery as well.

Thus the classification of the hulls and engines of all new vessels was for the first time made interdependent—a turning point in the history of shipping in general and of Lloyd's Register in particular. In the Register Book of 1879 there appeared a new notation, MS in red, denoting vessels classed in respect of machinery and periodically inspected. By 1884 engineer surveyors formed more than one-third of the Society's technical staff in the United Kingdom, and 26 engineering appointments had been made abroad.

*   *   *   *   *

This rapid growth merely anticipated another period of change, for even as Lloyd's Register had taken to classifying machinery and had not long finalised its Rules for the construction of iron ships, iron was being replaced by steel. Indeed, iron had been almost completely superseded by steel as the material mostly used in shipbuilding by 1888, barely ten years after the introduction of the latter substance for that purpose. It had taken nearly 50 years to put the iron ship on the map, so to speak, and it rapidly disappeared once the superior qualities of the stronger metal had been demonstrated.

Even a small schoolboy hardly needs to be told that steel was not a novelty in 1880 or thereabouts. He has read in his history books and romances that the knights of old were armoured in steel, and that the most lethal blades were made of the stuff. The production of steel on a large scale for industrial purposes was a discovery of the marvellous 19th Century, and when it was shown that plates of steel made a better ship than plates of iron, the forge industry flourished and expanded in the natural rhythm of commerce, the largest merchant fleet of all the nations requiring the resources of a huge industry.

The approach to the use of steel for shipbuilding purposes was gradual enough, and Lloyd's Register faced the development with an open mind but with characteristic caution. The Barrow Haematite Steel Company first brought the matter before the Society as early as 1866 when, it having been proposed that a vessel of 1,552 tons should be built of this Lancashire product, they suggested that four experienced surveyors of Lloyd's Register should visit the works and conduct experiments on the steel produced there. It had been urged that the vessel to be built of Barrow haematite steel should be allowed scantlings of one-third less in sectional area than those required in iron ships, but the surveyors sent to the Barrow district reported cautiously, and the Committee ultimately recommended:—

> "That ships built of steel of approved quality under Special Survey should be classed in the Register Book with the notation of 'Experimental' against their characters. The specifications for the ships must, however, be submitted to the Committee for approval.
> "That a reduction be allowed in the thickness of the plates, frames, etc., of ships built of steel, not exceeding one-fourth from that prescribed in Table G for Iron Ships. In other respects the Rules for the construction of Iron Ships will apply equally to Ships built of Steel.
> "That the steel must be equal to a tensile strain of not less than 30 tons to the square inch."

It must be put on record with due solemnity that the first vessel to receive a class under this arrangement was a small screw steamer with the blameless name of *Annie*, built by Samuelson of Hull in 1864. When classed under the new regulations three years later she was put into the category A1, according to the system of symbols then ruling, with the notations "(Steel)" and "Experimental".

Caution in regard to steel in the early years of its production on a commercial basis was wholly justified. The material was apt to be brittle and liable to fracture; and when it was really good, it could not compete with iron in price. After the first burst of interest in its possibilities steel was rather out of fashion for a decade, until improvements came with the introduction of the Bessemer and then the Siemens-Martin, or Open Hearth, processes. These made possible the production of a mild and ductile material at a greatly reduced cost; the new mild steel opened an era in shipbuilding development. Even the Admiralty, usually conservative, ordered its use in the construction of two cruisers towards the end of 1875. Technical bodies all over the country listened to the reading of papers on this exciting new subject, and steel works started to spring up in those parts of the country where the raw materials were at hand—Yorkshire, Durham, South Wales and Lanarkshire in particular.

Inevitably, thus, the Society faced the problems raised by what was currently called "the resurrection of steel", and the challenge came in 1877 when the shipbuilding firm of John Elder & Co. of Govan, pioneers of multiple expansion, gave proper notice that it proposed to use Siemens-Martin steel in the building of two cross-Channel packets, paddle-driven, for the London, Brighton and South Coast Railway Company—of happy memory. This was met calmly, the Society proposing a general reduction of 20 per cent in the thickness of plating, frames, etc., from those laid down in Table G for iron ships, stipulating only that periodical tests of the material to be used should be carried out from time to time under the personal supervision of its surveyors.

The inevitability of the replacement of iron by steel was accepted without fuss, and the caution of the Society's approach to the new problem is now seen to have been wholly wise. It was in fact really not very difficult to deal with the steel ship after so many years of agonising over the right rules for construction in iron. In 1885 Benjamin Martell as Chief Surveyor was set the task of drafting rules and tables of scantlings for the classification of steel vessels. This involved some special technical issues. For example, the introduction of mild steel in place of iron allowed a reduction of about 25 per cent in boiler scantlings, so that a general increase in steam pressures and a resultant economy in fuel consumption followed.

The new Rules for Steel Ships duly appeared in November, 1888. Over and above the allowances for reduced scantlings, these rules were interesting for their insistence on the importance of the quality of the steel now to be used in such huge quantities. Additional surveyors were appointed to test steel in the process of manufacture, and in some cases these officers were in constant attendance at the larger works, of which the Society issued an approved list.

The regulations had to be revised more than once during the bustling 1890's, and Lloyd's Register had much to do with, for example, the evolution of sound designs for the construction of new vessels. The technical experts had even to step aside to work out special rules for the construction of "turret deck" ships. These were designed largely to reduce the tolls payable on passages through the Suez Canal, then calculated in terms of deck space. The "turret" ships, much favoured by a number of shipowners trading mainly in merchandise to and from the Far East, thus took on the appearance of outsize submarines, the measurable deck space above their bulbous sides little more than a series of cat-walks.

The Rules for Steel Ships framed in 1888 endured with only minor modifications until 1909, and they thus covered almost exactly the span of a phase of fantastically rapid development in shipbuilding-engineering. As for machinery pure and simple, the quadruple expansion engine was first installed in a vessel in 1890; and only seven years were to pass before Charles Parsons first demonstrated the great possibilities of the steam turbine as applied to marine propulsion. Passenger vessels grew in size and power and speed—the three basic factors in the same theorem—and the propellers increased in number, two, three and four. The time had come when the transatlantic liner could have carried Henry Bell's pioneer *Comet* on its boat-deck without inconvenience.

The urge towards size and speed, to the point at which the latter consideration became a fetish, sprang mainly out of intense competition in the passenger trade between Europe and North America. This was competition on two levels, so to speak.

On the lower of these the trade was in emigrants. Those were the days when Canada in particular was taking in population as fast as it could find it and advertising all over Europe the extent and potential wealth of the prairie. The doors of the United States were still open, and neither that country nor its northern neighbour lacked for aspirants to citizenship. We all read nowadays of the departure of the occasional ship for Australia or New Zealand with selected settlers, but the occasion is rare enough to inspire a newspaper story and a photograph, and it amounts to a mere trickle compared with the flood that poured across the Atlantic about the turn of the century: the artisan seekers after high wages, the peasant from the "have not" countries of Europe, and not a few who, in the old phrase rarely heard nowadays, "left their country for their country's good". It is strange to remember how many bad boys of the British aristocracy and middle classes were in this fashion disposed of in remote parts.

Many artists, James Tissot among them, were inspired to paint the scene any Saturday forenoon on the piers of Liverpool and Greenock about the turn of the century—hordes of patient, hopeful persons, many in the long blue blouses and high boots of the Russian and Baltic peasantries, their womenfolk in voluminous black wrappings, waiting for the gangways to come down or the tender to take them out to the waiting ships—two or three or four every Saturday, Montreal- or New York-bound. One recalls the posters of the Allan and Donaldson Lines that advertised single steerage passages from the Clyde to Quebec at £7 and less a head: passengers to carry their own enamelled mugs, plates and primitive cutlery.

This trade did not inspire the production of any notably large or fine ships, though the average emigrant vessel of the period was usually a sturdy job, perfectly fit for its purpose. The splendour— one had almost said, the swank—came out of the competition for the much more expensive passenger trade between the terminal ports of the United Kingdom and Northern Europe on the one hand and New York on the other. This was a particularly lucrative trade, in that the owners of the swiftly increasing wealth of the United States were strongly impelled by powerful instincts and social aspirations to visit the ancestral Europe, to see Naples and die. This demand ordained the supply of ever larger, ever faster, ever more luxurious liners.

The story should be familiar. The competition ran on national lines, even to the extent of State subsidies for the competing shipping companies. One typical expression of it was the determined bid of Germany, with only a short coastline but a vast hinterland and vaster imperial ambitions, to dominate the route. Some journalist unhappily coined the phrase, "the Blue Riband of the Atlantic"—a blatant appeal at once to patriotism and vague sporting instincts; another the term "ocean greyhound". The biggest ship across the North Atlantic in the shortest time—that was the ruling notion: though why any rational person should want to shorten the blessed relaxation of an ocean voyage by a couple of hours is another question.

There it was, however: the nations panting after the mythical Blue Riband, now the British and now the Germans ahead, with the French and the Dutch and the Scandinavians intervening and the Italians running their own sleek ships out of the Mediterranean to the New World. Oddly enough, the Americans, with all their great technical skill and respectable seafaring tradition, entered the lists only spasmodically.

It was altogether such a marvellous phase of expansion that Lloyd's Register could not but be heavily involved in its implications. When the Cunard Company was considering in 1903 whether or not to install turbine machinery in two ships to be built in agreement with H.M. Government, it approached the Committee with the request that the Society's Chief Engineer Surveyor, James T. Milton, be allowed to serve on a board of inquiry into the advisability of the scheme. The result was the decision to engine with steam turbines the ill-fated *Lusitania* and the brilliant *Mauretania*. These large express passenger ships were built under the Society's special survey, and some of the most experienced officers of Lloyd's Register were lent to the Cunard Company to act exclusively as superintendents on behalf of the owners throughout the construction of these great vessels on the Clyde and Tyne respectively.

The vogue of the giant fast liner had its last logical expression in the two Cunard "Queens" of the 1930's. After the Second World War the Americans produced in the *United States*, a ship which, though not so large as the "Queens", is certainly faster, and the Blue Riband is now among the trophies of the States.

*   *   *   *   *

The middle of the period that has thus been reviewed in outline saw a remarkable development, a breakaway that seriously threatened the established authority of Lloyd's Register. As we see it now in the calm light of history, the seeds of this revolt were latent in several of the issues already accounted for and even in solutions or compromises agreed to, more or less willingly, by the Society.

The British Corporation was formed in Glasgow in 1890, and it was formidably backed. Virtually all the leading shipowners on the Clyde and many, but not all, of the larger shipbuilders in that area united in its founding, and they were not slow in stating that their rebellion was against certain rules and requirements approved by the Board of Trade and Lloyd's Register—or, in one way of looking at it, against lack of rules.

The Clyde had become the most productive shipbuilding area in the world and was then, by common consent, the most progressive; and no doubt these Scottish shipbuilders felt they knew a thing or two hidden from the pundits in London. Their movement, however, quickly attracted important adherents, and the British Corporation came to be strongly represented in Belfast, in Liverpool and Birkenhead (a separate Liverpool Committee was formed in 1912), on the Tyne and the Wear, with powerful support from Sweden. The chairman was a redoubtable character, Sir Nathaniel Dunlop of the Allan Line, and the movement had the strong support and skilled advice of Philip Jenkins, Professor of Naval Architecture in the University of Glasgow. It is notable that the Corporation represented mainly an alliance between shipbuilders and shipowners, and that the underwriter was hardly in the picture.

The ostensible cause of revolt in the first place was dissatisfaction with the ambiguous state in which the load line problem had been left by the ordinances of the mid-1880's. The Corporation appreciated the work Lloyd's Register had done in working out its tables of "reserve buoyancy", but its members were disturbed by the Board of Trade's declaration in 1886 that it did not intend to assign any more load lines. They remembered the absorption of the Liverpool Register into the body of Lloyd's Register, and they did not hesitate to express their fear that freeboard administration might become the latter's "monopoly"; nor need there be any suspicion that these northern shipping men were inspired by anything but their own strong feelings, born of practical experience, as to what constituted the proper factors of safety.

Their representations were powerful enough to impress the Board of Trade which, at the last minute, accepted two amendments to the

Merchant Shipping Act of 1890. These, in effect, removed the possibility of Lloyd's Register having a monopoly in the matter of freeboard assignment (if it had ever thought of claiming one) and allowed the existence of "any other approved Corporation for the survey and registry of shipping". The Register Committee of the British Corporation thus received appointment on October 28th, 1890, and proceeded immediately to incorporation.

Other ideas, or ideals, of the founders of the British Corporation are rather highly technical in character. They were much concerned, for example, with the design of cargo-carrying space, seeking to eliminate beams and stringers that could interfere with the handling of goods, and thus allow for comparatively light scantlings; and one of their printed manifestos had a cunning side-kick at Lloyd's Register, with a reference to outmoded notions based on sailing ship practice, or words to that effect.

Any reader sufficiently interested in such technical niceties can easily find access to them in any respectable reference library. For the purely historical record, the British Corporation published its first Register Book and Rules in 1893. Fifty owners had submitted for classification 463 vessels with a total tonnage of 985,000, and the growth was regular thereafter. The Corporation had a fine record throughout the 57 years of its life, and its technicians contributed valuably to the evolution of the modern ship. In it Lloyd's Register had certainly a formidable rival.

The breach was to be closed eventually, but that event will fall into place in due course.

CHAPTER 8   INTO THE 20TH CENTURY

THE period between the end of the South African War in 1902 and the outbreak of the First World War in 1914 is generally regarded as a sort of golden age in British history; and so it may have been in the social sense. The rigid respectability of Victoria's domination cracked under the warm influence of a second Merry Monarch. Money abounded, and money either inherited or earned was affected by neither heavy taxation nor devaluation. Cheerfulness and confidence informed the British people, and it was indeed a good time to live in for those above the poverty line.

It is easy now to be wise after the event, but there must have been some contemporary students of history to worry not a little over the signs and portents. The Lloyd George Budget of 1909, with its imposition of death duties on a heavy scale, and the constitutional crisis of 1911 clearly pointed to a changing Shape of Things to Come. Within the special field of shipping that is our concern here—always remembering that shipping is a prime expression of the British genius—there were many growths to disturb the watcher.

The Admiralty's decision to base the country's naval defence mainly on great battleships of the Dreadnought class, to be followed by the equally powerful and faster battle-cruisers, was portentous; and so were the unresting efforts of the subsidised merchant fleet of Germany to secure and hold that rather tedious honour, the Blue Riband of the Atlantic. The great passenger liners grew bigger and faster, and the catastrophe of the *Titanic* in 1912 might have been seen to be ominous. The Cunard Company's *Aquitania* of 1914 was 869 feet in length, and Germany retorted in the same year with the *Vaterland*, 907 feet in length. All these spectacular events apart, however, the period between 1900 and 1914 is seen in terms of shipping history, and therefore in those applicable to Lloyd's Register of Shipping, to have been momentous in directions that, taken for granted in 1960 by the plain citizen, were remarkable at the time only to the specialists. For example our forefathers were slow to realise the importance of refrigeration.

The interest of inventive persons in refrigeration was first confined to ways and means of keeping perishable goods fresh in store. Machines for making ice, apparatus for freezing by the evaporation of a volatile liquid, and the reduction of temperatures by the use of cooled air—the patents were numerous from 1824 onwards; and the first freezing works in the world were set up in Sydney, N.S.W. in 1861, by Thomas Mort. It was quite another problem to discover how freezing machinery could be installed and kept working within the hull of a ship at sea. At last two ingenious Frenchmen, Tellier and Carré, succeeded, though separately, wonderfully well in transporting cargoes of meat across the oceans: Tellier's little steamer bearing the splendidly cogent name of *Frigorifique*. The machinery involved, however, the use of ammonia, and any leakage of that substance was dangerous as well as unpleasant, as an Australian, James Harrison, discovered when he made a ruinous experiment in transporting a cargo of meat in the ship *Norfolk*, using a mixture of ice and salt in two tanks.

That was in 1877; and in the same year a Glasgow firm interested in the matter, Henry & James Bell, sensibly took the problem to that remarkable man, Sir William Thomson, later Lord Kelvin, for so many years a professor at Glasgow University. Thomson's advice was that the question should be passed on to a chemist of promise, Joseph Coleman; and this young man produced in due course what came to be called the Bell-Coleman machine, in which compressed air could be so used as to produce low temperatures.

The first experimental installation was built into the Anchor liner *Circassia* in 1879 and proved a success. In 1880 the *Strathleven*, equipped with the Bell-Coleman equipment, delivered in London a sound cargo of frozen meat from Australia. Two years later a sailing ship, the *Dunedin*, of that Albion Line which was subsequently absorbed in the Shaw Savill organisation, carried the first cargo of frozen meat from New Zealand to Britain.

It was all so exciting in the popular view that *Punch* was moved to publish a cartoon depicting Jack Frost as the universal provider of the future. Lloyd's Register, however, did not at once see the problem of refrigeration as coming within its province. But as the value of these shipments increased during the 1880's and it was seen that underwriters might sustain inordinately heavy losses in the case of mechanical failure, the Society decided in 1898 that the inspection of refrigerating machinery was indeed its business. An engineer surveyor on the staff, Robert Balfour, presented a report on the subject; and when rules had been framed on that basis, he became the Society's first Refrigerating Engineer.

The Rules, published in the last month of 1898, were at once elaborate and cautious in the now familiar way of Lloyd's Register, but they were warmly welcomed by shipowners, especially since the appropriate certificate could be granted in respect of refrigeration alone to a vessel otherwise unclassed. The selected notation was ✠ RMC—that is, Refrigerating Machinery Certificate—a notation amended in 1910, to ✠ Lloyd's RMC. As "chilled" meat and dairy produce were added to the list of refrigerated goods the Society's work in this field rapidly increased. By 1906 the number of ships classed ✠ RMC had grown to 108, with a total carrying capacity of some ten million carcases. An enlarged staff of surveyors with experience in refrigeration had to be set up at Buenos Aires. Soon enough the Society had undertaken responsibility for the periodical

G

inspection of cold stores on land and, as requested by the Port of London Authority, of the fleet of insulated barges on the River Thames.

The First World War dramatically emphasised the importance of refrigeration, as we shall see, but before that critical period was reached the Society and its experts were faced with a large set of problems—those represented by oil in its various aspects. To the experts of Lloyd's Register the subject sooner or later presented three different aspects, thus:—(a) the carriage of oil in ships from distant wells; (b) the use of oil as a substitute for coal in firing ships' boilers, and (c) its use as a fuel in the internal combustion engine as a means of propulsion.

The early history of oil-carrying is, like that of refrigeration, faintly comic in modern eyes. In the first place, of course, the stuff was carried across the sea in barrels, as it might have been molasses or beer. The need for vessels specially designed for the purpose was realised in the 1860's, however, when Lloyd's Register had to consider plans for three vessels in that character—the *Atlantic* and the *Great Western*, built by Rogerson & Co. on the Tyne, and the *Ramsey* built in—of all improbable places—the Isle of Man. These three ships were sailing vessels, and the best their designers could do for the carriage of oil was to divide the hold space by a bulkhead along the centre line, with transverse bulkheads forming eight compartments of 20 feet in length each. There is no evidence that any ever carried a gallon of oil. Soon after their completion all were happily engaged in general cargo trade.

Three sizeable steam vessels of the early 1870's—the *Vaderland*, the *Netherland* and the *Switzerland*, all out of Palmer's Tyneside yard—showed a considerable advance in design for the given purpose of oil-carrying in bulk. In these cases there was at least an approach to the idea, so obvious to-day, of embodying the tanks in the vessel's fabric instead of separating them entirely from the shell. They were intended to carry oil from the United States to Belgium, and they were granted the Society's classification, but again a sensible project got confused in a comedy of errors.

In the first place, the Belgian authorities refused to allow storage tanks to be built for the warehousing of the inflammable cargoes, and the American authorities refused to licence the ships for the carriage of passengers. When the *Vaderland* arrived at Philadelphia to lift her first cargo of oil, the pumping apparatus was not ready, and the owners accepted a more profitable general cargo. The results of this unexpected deal were so satisfactory that all three ships were put to general trading and, with the extra inducement of a mail contract from the Belgian Government, the owners conveniently forgot their first intention.

The development of critical value came in 1886, when Armstrong, Mitchell & Co. built on the Tyne the *Gluckauf* of 2,307 tons and the old firm of Wm. Gray & Co. of West Hartlepool put into the water within the same week the *Bakuin*. The latter was classed ✠100A1 in the Register Book, with the notation "Carrying Petroleum in Bulk". In both these vessels the designers used the outer shell of the ship as the skin of the tank, so to speak; and in the case of a third vessel of the same year, the *Loutsch* from the yard of Hawthorn, Leslie & Co., the oil was carried up to the underside of the weather deck. The *Bakuin* was in constant service and regular classification until broken up in September, 1902, and the *Loutsch*, latterly *Chaumian*, was believed to be going strong in Russian hands until 1950 at least.

These were the first real "tankers". Oddly enough, a number of older ships of conventional type were converted to oil-carrying during the 1880's, and the necessary surveys were carried out by the Society's experts. The critical change in the shipbuilder's approach to this special problem came early in the 20th Century.

Joseph Isherwood entered the Society's service at West Hartlepool as a young ship surveyor in 1896. He was soon transferred to London, there to work on plans in the department of the Chief Ship Surveyor, still the indestructible Benjamin Martell. The lad was clearly a naval architect of outstanding parts; and in due course, his qualities feeding on the vast amount of material accumulated in the archives of Lloyd's Register, he evolved what is now known as the Isherwood System. This was an invention, and Isherwood took out a patent. He submitted his proposals to the Committee, and read an important paper before the Institution of Naval Architects, but he also resigned from the Society's service in order, quite legitimately, to devote the whole of his time to the commercial development of his patent.

Isherwood's plan cut right across the traditional pattern of design.

It substituted longitudinal for lateral framing; that is, roughly, the ship's ribs ran fore and aft instead of from side to side at intervals. Its application made it possible to calculate the strength of a ship's structure with a larger freedom from initial assumptions than had been possible in terms of tradition. The girders running fore and aft had the valuable effect of reinforcing the thinner plating of decks; and the system allowed considerable saving in material. For his great contribution to specialised ship design Joseph Isherwood received the honour of a baronetcy.

The first ship to be built on the Isherwood plan was the *Paul Paix*, on the Tees in 1908. Isherwood had been trained in Lloyd's Register, but his ideas appealed strongly to the rival British Corporation. So the construction of the *Paul Paix* was overseen by surveyors of both Lloyd's Register and the British Corporation, and the ship was classed with both Societies. Lloyd's Register duly classed the *Paul Paix* with the now familiar notation, "Longitudinal Framing"; and in 1909 it issued its separate Rules for the construction of vessels intended for the carriage of petroleum in bulk. But that was long before both shipping and oil concerns came to contemplate the building of tankers the size of large passenger liners.

The use of oil for firing boilers did not develop on a large scale until after the First World War, and the phase will be dealt with in its proper place, but it is well to understand now the point of development reached before the tragic struggle of 1914–18 changed the world the comfortable Edwardians had known. Once again, the story has its comic aspects.

The first step towards the use of oil as a fuel in marine boilers followed the exploitation of the oilfields on a commercial basis. That was in 1859 or thereabouts. The fuels available were varied—for instance, "Astaki", a residue oil from South Russia, heavy shale oil from the Lothians of Scotland, and ordinary creosote. All these substances were heavy by modern standards, but inventive man soon enough evolved a type of burner in which the viscous materials could be atomised by injections of steam. In 1885 the Society was invited to deal with the case of the steamer *Himalaya* which, already classed, had been bought by the Marahu Petroleum & Oil Produce Co. for the express purpose of experimenting with a steam-injection burner of this type. The fuel was Scotch shale oil, carried in barrels on deck, and one of the Society's surveyors was sent to keep his eyes open during the trial voyage from London to the Firth of Forth and back. He was not impressed, and that sort of installation was abandoned.

The next experiment was made in 1887 with the *Charles Howard*, converted under the Society's inspection for both the carriage of oil in bulk and for burning oil as fuel. This was carried in the ship's double bottom, but the Committee would not have it that sufficient precaution had been taken against leakage, and the vessel's classification was withdrawn. In the issue the oil-firing apparatus broke down before the ship reached Gibraltar. The owners were glad to return to the use of coal, and the ship's former classification was restored in the next edition of the Register Book.

There were other experiments, more or less successful, but for many years the Society stuck to its point that these installations were "experimental". The Rules ultimately prepared were severe.

They considered, for a start, the problem of how steam was to be supplied to the burners and the ship's supply of fresh water kept to an adequate level at the same time. Each fuel compartment was to be well ventilated and strong enough to withstand the surge of oil within a half-empty tank in rough weather. Pumps for moving or pressurising oil were to be installed within a chamber separated from the machinery space by gas-tight bulkheads, this to be both naturally and mechanically ventilated, and access to it was to be provided from the deck.

The low flash-points of the fuels available in those early days formed, of course, the complete justification of the Society's stringency. Man learned, however, how to use low flash oil; and to all that this narrative will return in due course.

As for the use of oil in internal combustion engines for the purpose of propulsion, that stems largely from the discovery by Rudolf Diesel, born in Paris of German parents and fated to a mysterious death in the North Sea, that heavy oil could be used to produce power for heavy work as the explosion of vaporised petrol impels the pistons of a motor-car's engine. The invention has proved so revolutionary that it is commonplace nowadays to refer to a diesel engine, without the grace of a capital letter. Not that all the credit can go to Diesel; British engineers, notably Ackroyd Stuart working for the Crossley concern, had experimented valuably in the same field.

The discovery made and the efficiency of the engine demonstrated, the shipbuilder-engineers of Europe and America hastened to use it for their own urgent purposes; and they were, so to speak, batting on an easy wicket. Most of the problems of design, stresses and transmission as affecting ship's hulls had been worked out by often bitter trial and error in relation to the steam engine. The replacement of steam by oil involved, to be sure, certain special considerations—notably the cooling arrangements essential in such an installation, the unknown factor of stresses set up by heat, and the problems of reversing. In the nature of things the applications of Dr. Diesel's invention immediately engaged the interest of Lloyd's Register and its experts.

The then Chief Engineer Surveyor, Dr. James T. Milton, was despatched to consult the leading specialists in oil engine construction in the United Kingdom and on the Continent, conferring with the great Diesel himself. The fruits of his inquiries were embodied in two papers that, read before the Institution of Civil Engineers and the Institution of Naval Architects respectively, excited much professional interest and provoked a good deal of useful argument. In 1910 the Society issued its first Rules for petrol and paraffin engines—a move of rather unusual interest, indicating the fact that such engines were being increasingly used in small craft. The Society's British and American Yacht Registers for that year testify that some of these engines were of considerable size.

The first ocean-going motorship to receive classification from Lloyd's Register was the *Vulcanus*, built by the Nederlandsche Scheepsbouw Maatschappij of Amsterdam in 1910 for the Nederlandsch-Indische Tankstoomboot Maatschappij. The first motorship built in the United Kingdom, by Barclay, Curle & Co. in 1912, was the *Jutlandia*, classed by the British Corporation.

The East Asiatic Company, a venerable Danish concern, led the movement towards the general use of oil engines in quite large vessels. They had the *Selandia* and the *Fionia* of 5,000 tons each, sisters to the *Jutlandia* but built and engined by Burmeister & Wain of Copenhagen; and these were so successful that several British, Dutch and Swedish firms followed the lead. The engines were 4-stroke cycle single-acting jobs, using heavy oil . . . and the layman need not be dismayed by the nomenclature of a period of experiment. One pioneer ship built under the special survey of Lloyd's Register, the *Holzapfel I*, was fitted with suction gas engines using anthracite as fuel. It is important only to appreciate the fact that all the experimental engines of the period were of some sort of internal combustion type, requiring no boilers for raising steam, working economically on the explosion of hydro-carbon gases within their cylinders.

A major advance in this field stands to the credit of a British firm, Wm. Doxford & Sons, of Sunderland. Even after the First World War had broken out, they introduced a 2-stroke opposed piston engine. This engine was subjected to an exhaustive shop trial lasting $34\frac{1}{2}$ days, surveyors of Lloyd's Register in attendance. In that year, 1914, the Society published its first Rules for the construction and survey of diesel engines and their auxiliaries.

As the Clyde had led in the development of the steam engine, so the rivers of North-Eastern England pioneered successfully in the matter of the heavy oil engine; and this has had one odd little consequence on the human side. As Kipling recorded, the predominant voice in any ship's engineroom during the age of steam was that of Macandrew. In the age of the motorship it is that of Geordie and his neighbours. And when boilers were still fired by coal, it needed more than 100 firemen to keep the furnaces going in a large passenger liner, such as the *Mauretania*. The same work can be done by perhaps 30 men tending oil burners.

The larger developments of these new forces in the fields of refrigeration and oil had to await the end of the First World War, that Great Divide in the lives of millions of people and the fates of several nations. It is convenient, however, to take 1914 as a mile post in the story of such an institution as Lloyd's Register; and it is fitting to pause here and consider how the Society had fared on the administrative and domestic side before the lights went out all over Europe.

*   *   *   *   *

It is remarkable that during the eight decades between 1834 and the outbreak of the First World War the highest places within Lloyd's Register were occupied by relatively few men, each with a long record of service: a testimony at once to the toughness of our forefathers and to the justice of the Society's dealings with its most trusted servants.

As we have seen, the distinguished Thomas Chapman, with such a fine head and face as any artist would have loved to paint, held office as Chairman over the long period from 1835 to 1881, steering a vessel with certain weak parts through stormy seas to security. His successor, William Henry Tindall, admirably discharged the difficult task of filling the shoes of an outstanding personality. Having joined the Committee as early as 1856, his knowledge of the Society's affairs was exhaustive, and he had the gifts of geniality and tact: qualities very desirable when it came to handling such matters as the amalgamation with the Underwriters' Registry, and the framing of the first Load Line regulations and the first Rules for Steel Ships.

Here is a full list of Chairmen of the Society since 1834:

1834–1835	David Carruthers
1835–1881	Thomas Chapman, F.R.S., F.S.A.
1881–1899	William Henry Tindall
1899–1907	Sir John Glover
1907–1909	James Dixon
1909–1920	Sir Thomas Lane Devitt, Bart.
1921	Sir John Henry Luscombe
1922–1925	James Herbert Scrutton
1925–1928	Sir Thomas James Storey, K.B.E.
1928–1943	Sir George Higgins, C.B.E.
1943–1946	Ernest Lionel Jacobs
1946–1957	Sir Ronald Thornbury Garrett
1957 to present day	Kenneth Raymond Pelly, M.C.

On the Staff side Bernard Waymouth, having been Principal Surveyor for two years from 1871, flourished as Secretary until he died in harness in 1890. His successor as Chief Surveyor, Benjamin Martell—a man of short stature, affectionately known to shipbuilders throughout the country as "Little Benjamin, our Ruler"—did not retire until 1900; and Waymouth's successor as Secretary, Arthur G. Dryhurst, was in that onerous position until 1904. The first Principal, then Chief, Engineer Surveyor, William Parker, served the Society faithfully for 16 years until 1890; and his successor, Dr. James T. Milton, was in command of that important, and increasingly important, department until 1921.

We see that longevity and an ability to rub along with others characterised the original stalwarts of Lloyd's Register in a remarkable degree; and the social historian might observe with interest how this probably reflected the stability of a period of expansion. The temptation to reason in the same way about the rather more frequent changes in the Chair and other high offices after the turn of the century should, however, be resisted. First of all, and rather obviously, it became increasingly difficult for any man engaged in large-scale modern commerce to give to the Society's affairs such utter devotion as Chapman and Tindall had contrived to do. More significantly, the bases of the Society's constitution were greatly extended between 1900 and 1914.

The first movement in this direction took place in 1900, when the Glasgow Committee was formed. If this was in some sort a retort to the inauguration of the British Corporation there, it recognised the great importance of the Clyde in shipping affairs, and it brought into the counsels of the Society many able men. This Branch Committee, consisting of 15 members, was representative of the Glasgow Underwriters' Association, the Glasgow Chamber of Commerce, the Glasgow Shipowners' Association, the Greenock Chamber of Commerce and other bodies. (At least one of these, the Clyde Sailing Shipowners' Association is, like the fine ships they put upon the seas, no more.)

The larger expansion involved the admission of shipbuilders to the General Committee, at length. This move had been under consideration for many years. It is true that some shipbuilders had served on the Committee from time to time, but not *qua* shipbuilders, only as they were also merchants or shipowners, or underwriters to some extent. As far back as the 1880's a leading counsel had advised the Society that the constitution of 1834 was inviolable: that the Committee could consist only of Merchants, Shipowners and Underwriters. Though it may seem to us nowadays a quibble, especially considering the enormous influence of shipbuilding in the affairs with which Lloyd's Register was most vitally concerned, it was not until 1890 that the thin end of the wedge was fashioned. This was the formation of a technical Sub-Committee, to consist partly of Members of the General Committee and partly of representative shipbuilders and marine engineers. The election of the latter was left to three bodies—the Institution of Naval Architects in London, the Institution of Shipbuilders and Engineers of the North-East Coast of

England in Newcastle upon Tyne, and the Institution of Engineers and Shipbuilders in Scotland, in Glasgow.

Each of these institutions was to elect two shipbuilders and two engineers to form a technical reserve, so to call it, but none was to sit on the General Committee. The advance produced notably satisfactory results in the way of keeping the Society and its various sets of Rules abreast of current techniques, and to this Sub-Committee representatives of the steelmakers and forgemasters were subsequently added with equally valuable results. A rather ludicrous state of affairs remained, however, and late in 1909 the Society went back to eminent counsel who, cheerfully reversing the opinions of their learned brethren of 50 years before, declared unequivocally that the Committee could safely extend its field of representation to render the greatest possible service to the shipping community.

The extremely important upshot of these proceedings was that, at a Special Meeting of the General Committee in June, 1911, it was resolved that ten representatives, shipbuilders and/or engineers, should be added to its number.

The Society had in the meantime been in occupation since 1901 of a great office building of its own. Towards the end of the 19th Century it had become obvious that the premises at No. 2, White Lion Court, leased from the Merchant Taylors Company, could no longer accommodate the expanding staff, even if two extra storeys had been put up to house it. A freehold site in Fenchurch Street was therefore secured in November, 1897, and T. E. Collcutt, F.R.I.B.A., was commissioned to design a building to match the size and dignity of Lloyd's Register of British and Foreign Shipping. The work of building was delayed for various reasons, and it was not until December 19th, 1901, that the Committee met in the new Board Room.

This is an impressive chamber. Quite apart from the painted ceiling by Gerald Moira, the marble columns in the Numidian style and the fine inlaid panelling in African mahogany, it wears the air of old dignity in the rows of Committee seats under the Chairman's rostrum, the portraits of past Chairmen looking gravely down on the proceedings of their successors. No. 71, Fenchurch Street may not be the modern architect's notion of a "functional" building, but its interior has a charm appropriate to its ancient lineage, from the decorum of the uniformed servants to the enormous volumes of wood in the swing doors, decorated with brass handles as ponderous as the embellishments of an admiral's barge.

Here, then, Lloyd's Register was well settled to face the crowding problems and the gross overwork of the First World War. The Chairman in August, 1914, was the distinguished shipowner, Sir Thomas Devitt, Bart.; his Deputy-Chairman was Sir Frederic Bolton. The Chief Ship Surveyor was Westcott S. Abell, latterly Sir Westcott Abell, K.B.E., who had just succeeded Dr. Samuel Thearle. The Chief Engineer Surveyor was still Dr. James T. Milton, and the Secretary was Andrew Scott, afterwards Sir Andrew, who had succeeded Arthur G. Dryhurst in 1904. It was a good team.

It was in this year that the Society simplified its title. Since 1834 it had been known as Lloyd's Register of British and Foreign Shipping, but not long before the outbreak of the First World War the epithets were seen to be superfluous. The shortened title had the effect of emphasising the international character of the institution.

CHAPTER 9   FOUR YEARS OF WAR

A T the outbreak of war in 1914 the Society's staff consisted of 360
surveyors and rather more than 100 workers on the administrative side. Many of these volunteered at once for active service, and when the resources of Lloyd's Register were placed unreservedly at the disposal of the British and Allied Governments, several members of the technical staffs had to be withdrawn from the Services. Many members of Committees were called upon to take leading parts in the control of merchant shipping and shipbuilding in one or other of the departments set up to handle these critical concerns. In particular, the Merchant Shipbuilding Advisory Committee set up by the Shipping Controller, Sir Joseph (later Lord) Maclay, made extensive use of the Society's organisation and resources and co-opted its Chief Ship Surveyor, Westcott Abell, as a member. Abell was latterly appointed

Technical Adviser to the Controller of Shipping and for his brilliant work was created Knight Commander of the British Empire.

In the early stages of the conflict the Society's surveyors had special duties over and above that of surveying and classifying merchant vessels at home and abroad. The special survey during construction of ships for the Admiralty and War Office; the inspection and testing of war material in the United States for the British Government; the inspection and testing in Great Britain of war material for the French Government, and the holding of condition surveys of both British and foreign ships requisitioned by the Allied Governments—these were among the extra burdens that had to be borne. The surveying staff of 360 in 1914 had by 1919 grown to 513, of whom 455 were exclusive officers of the Society.

This increase was accounted for by two special factors. Although the United States had not yet entered the war, by 1915 American yards had started to meet Allied needs for new shipping; and though the technical capacity of the Americans is superb, the industry over there had not evolved such a set of standards as Lloyd's Register had worked out during its long existence. More than that, the lack of skilled shipyard labour in the States called loudly for expert supervision. Then, when the U-boat threat became acute in 1916–17, the British industry had to turn to those rapid improvisations already mentioned. In both these phases the Society and its officers were deeply involved.

Lloyd's Register was firmly established on the American scene in 1916. As an outcome of negotiations carried out by the Society's Secretary, Andrew Scott, an American Committee was established in New York, underwriters, shipowners, shipbuilders and engineers sitting under the chairmanship of Alfred Gilbert Smith, President of the New York and Cuba Mail Steamship Company. From this country Mr. James French, formerly the Society's Principal Surveyor at Glasgow, was sent out to be Chief Surveyor for the United States and Canada and Technical Adviser to the American Committee, and he was given powers to make his own decisions on the spot. He was followed by Mr. H. A. Ruck-Keene, then an assistant to the Society's Chief Engineer Surveyor, Dr. James T. Milton, and his ultimate successor. His special task was the co-ordination of effort in the production of marine engines and boilers throughout establishments scattered over thousands of square miles of North American territory. The Society's technical staff in America had numbered 22 at the outbreak of war; it had grown to 124 by 1918.

American industry benefited greatly through the skills of the surveyors of Lloyd's Register, but it has to be acknowledged that the surveyors and, through them, the British shipbuilding industry learned much from the American ability in brilliant improvisation and the national capacity to face and solve huge problems of mass production.

Thus, by 1915, the Americans were applying the principle of pre-fabrication, finding much of the required material in bridge-building shops and putting it together in shipyards hastily laid out. It need hardly be explained that this process—always remembering the wideness of America's spaces—called for elaborate and meticulous planning, and a vast proliferation of copies of plans for different types of ships, so that the bits and pieces from scores of widely separate sources could be put together with jigsaw precision at the place of assembly. The most spectacular feat of American engineering was the *ad hoc* creation of the legendary shipyard at Hog Island, Pennsylvania, where a frozen marsh was thawed, reclaimed and turned within a few months into a tidy unit for the rapid assembly of ships in 50 berths. At one time 30 of the Society's surveyors were kept hard at work in this single establishment.

One aspect of American shipbuilding during the emergency must have pleased the traditionalists. This was the extensive use of wood in the construction of both merchant and auxiliary vessels of considerable size. The wood was on the spot in large quantities, and if it could not be seasoned, the practical American mind decided, and rightly, that it would serve temporary purposes to excellent effect. During the last year of the war 566 wooden ships—426 in the U.S.A. and 140 in Canada—added a million gross tons to the maritime resources of the Allies. It is a pleasing historical fact that most of these were built in accordance with the Society's Rules for Wood Ships.

This activity in North America had one odd extension. The young of 1960 may not know that Japan was on the Allied side in that conflict, but she was not called upon to make a serious naval contribution to the ultimate victory. On the other hand, her shipyards could make their contribution to the shipping pool, and most of the material required was produced in the United States. Upon James French, the Society's Chief Surveyor in North America, there was therefore thrown the additional responsibility of passing plans for construction in Japan.

This war period saw an immense, and immensely rapid, expansion of American shipbuilding capacity. In 1914 the total output of all the native yards was in the region of only about 200,000 gross tons. At the Armistice in November, 1918, there were operating in the United States 140 shipyards with a potential output of more than 3,500,000 gross tons. It could likewise be argued that when Britain ran into the grave shipping crisis of 1916–17 the situation was saved in part by the adoption of American methods of, or at least of American attitudes towards, mass production.

This had its most important expression in the Standard ship. It was an unlovely thing, this pantechnicon of the high seas, but it served its purpose of carrying the cargoes the Allies so desperately required, and its simplified, fixed design saved Britain much in the way of materials and labour and time. To help speed the production of these vessels the Society lent to the department of the Controller General of Merchant Shipbuilding, Lord Pirrie, the services of Dr. James Montgomerie, then Principal Surveyor for Scotland and later Chief Ship Surveyor, and his work as liaison officer earned high official commendation.

Towards the end of the war material for even the Standard ships became scarce, and passes were made at constructing ships out of reinforced concrete. These monstrosities had rather the air of floating swimming pools, but the Society dutifully appointed experts to act as surveyors. The Admiralty proposed to use them mainly as tugs and barges on the English Channel service, and they were duly classed by the Society with the special notation of "Subject to Annual Survey—Experimental".

A special problem that came to face the Society and its experts during the emergency was that of supervising, in yards hitherto engaged exclusively in the construction of merchant ships, the building of auxiliary naval vessels—notably those required for the anti-submarine campaign. Most of these craft had to be of shallow draught and they therefore required the lightest possible scantlings; and the requirement in its turn demanded the highest class of workmanship, a commodity in ever-diminishing supply. It was in a specialised field such as this that the vast accumulated experience of Lloyd's Register was of supreme national value, and assuredly the Admiralty alone could not have compassed the vast amount of skilled supervision and careful organisation required.

So far as round figures are impressive, more than 650,000 tons gross of shipping in this category passed under the inspection of Lloyd's Register. From 1914 to 1919 nearly 10,000,000 tons of new shipping in all categories were specially surveyed and classed.

The testing of metals of various sorts also demanded the services of large and skilled staffs. During the war years nearly 8,000,000 tons of steel for use in shipbuilding were dealt with by the Society's surveyors. Large quantities of condenser tubes, copper pipes, brass bars, strips and sheets, steel wires, hydrogen cylinders and so on were ordered in the States; and since the ship and engineer surveyors already there had their hands more than full, many additional officers had to be sent out from Britain. At the same time, the French Government ordered in this country large supplies of shell steel of the highest quality, and it was not easy to comply with the specification. Lloyd's Register, however, produced a team that assisted in doubling production to 10,000 tons a week within three years. Seventy surveyors were engaged on this single task when the work was at full pressure, passing altogether 1,400,000 tons of this high-quality steel for our Allies.

The task of tidying up after the war was a formidable one, but it involved certain important changes in the Society's functions and attitudes, and these, some of great interest, will be dealt with later on. London was a more peaceful place during that First World War than it was during the Second, and the work at Head Office, though heavy for the obvious reasons, was never seriously interrupted. Though almost all of them could have claimed to be in the class of "essential" and, as we have seen, many experts had to be reclaimed from the Services, 108 members of the staff saw active service, and 15 of these did not return.

The Society was singularly fortunate in that, despite the strains of the period, there was very little change in the ranks of higher responsibility. Sir Thomas Devitt remained Chairman until failing health compelled him to relinquish office in 1920. The Deputy-Chairman Sir Frederic Bolton, retired in 1917 and was succeeded by Sir Edward Ernest Cooper, afterwards Lord Mayor of London, 1919–1920. Among the senior officers of the Society the Secretary, Andrew Scott, the Chief Ship Surveyor, Westcott Abell, and the Chief Engineer Surveyor, James T. Milton, survived the gruelling course.

It is pleasant to be able to add that, without the Committee's knowledge, one of the Society's principal works was used during that First World War as an instrument in the shadowy game of counter-espionage. The story is told in "Indiscretions of a Naval Censor" by Rear-Admiral Sir Douglas Brownrigg, thus:—

> "There had been a considerable outcry from France concerning the lack of precaution in this country against the leakage of news of sinkings, etc., so that the circulation of Lloyd's Register was suspended as regards France as one possible channel of leakage, until there came a violent protest to the effect that the French Admirals could not do without it! So they had perforce to have it. Presently, we so restricted the information put into Lloyd's Register that it no longer retained its unbroken record of reliable figures, and it was with a very light heart that, on the signing of the Armistice, I sent out letters saying that they could revert to their pre-war practice. I would, if I did not feel utterly impenitent, apologise for having so harried the shipping authorities, but I believe they agreed with me that every step taken was intended to hamper the enemy, and to safeguard our shipping. At all events, the officials and staff of Lloyd's Register, as well as Lloyd's, co-operated with us most loyally throughout the War, and were really helpful."

The precautions do not appear, however, to have been completely effective. It is on record that copies of the Register for 1915–16 and for 1916–17 did somehow get through to Germany. There each page of nearly 1500 pages in each volume was patiently photographed for the German Admiralty and so for the special use of U-boat commanders. This was confirmed by the film captured from Germany and ultimately shown in this country as "The Adventures of U 34". In this document a German submarine officer is shown in the act of erasing from a page of the Register the name of a torpedoed merchant vessel. One hopes that the patient "posters" of the Book were thus vouchsafed a sense of the importance of their work.

H

CHAPTER 10   RECOVERY AND ADVANCE

THE pattern of industrial recovery from a great war is always the same. The first phase is that of reorganisation or, vulgarly but plainly, clearing up the mess. The second is that of restoration, or the switching of huge masses of machinery back to the normal functions. The third and most interesting stage is that of the development and application of new ideas either suggested by experience in war or retarded by the need to concentrate on lethal commodities. Reflecting exactly the moods of Britain's great shipbuilding industry, Lloyd's Register, its governors and its servants, experienced the whole gamut of consequences in the most intimate way after 1918.

Towards the end of the war the Society's strict Rules for the periodical survey of classed ships had had to be modified, for the good reasons that labour to open up ships for inspection was scarce, and that all the available surveyors were busy on more urgent tasks.

The Society's device in these circumstances was to suggest to owners of all classed vessels that these would be maintained in class if submitted to inspection of a general kind as opportunity offered and as their state and age suggested; but it was laid down at the same time that repairs recommended by the surveyors must be carried out, and that surveys of boilers and screw shafts must be made strictly as they fell due. Ships thus treated were given the special but rather non-committal notation of "Examined" along with the date in the Register Book.

This was to put off the evil day, of course, and it was long after the Armistice before the slack of systematic survey and reclassification was taken up. At the same time, the Society had been entrusted with the survey of vessels surrendered by Germany in terms of the capitulation. The quite considerable number of British ships that had been interned had to be dealt with. All the Governments concerned agreed that the Society should report on the many hundreds of ships taken over by the Ministry of Shipping from foreign owners and assess their condition before redelivery. Finally, when hostilities ended, some 5,000,000 tons of shipping were being built in various parts of the world under the Society's inspection for ultimate classification.

The period of reorganisation was long and difficult; and it was immediately followed—to a considerable extent overlapped—by that of restoration. As usual, the coming of peace was followed by a "boom" in trade. During the two years following the Armistice about 8,000,000 tons of merchant shipping were built to the Society's classification. It was good while it lasted, but the technicians of Lloyd's Register were by this time tired and overworked men, and in fact a depression was soon to follow.

This breather was accepted by the Committee as an opportunity of examining the Rules that had served the shipping community so long and so well but had been, to an extent not precisely calculable, affected by the international upheaval. The Chief Ship Surveyor, Sir Westcott Abell, was accordingly instructed to devote himself to a thorough consideration of the existing regulations in the light of changed circumstances. His proposals were duly considered by two technical sub-committees, and with slight modifications they were approved and adopted by the General Committee to take effect as from January 1st, 1923.

These revised Rules were a great improvement on those previously in force, especially in respect that they could be applied in a more flexible manner. The principle recognised was that, within limits, the scantlings of a ship should be based on its draught. Two sets of Tables covered two main classes of ships, thus:—

(a) The full scantling ship, with the maximum draught permitted by its dimensions in terms of the Load Line Regulations. Such ships were classed 100A1.

(b) The complete superstructure ship, in which the scantlings were adjusted to a freeboard appropriate to that of the open shelter-deck ship of the period. Such were classed 100A1 "with freeboard".

Even if the layman may be faintly baffled by the technicalities, he may easily understand that these new Rules were directly applicable to a whole range of sea-going vessels, since the scantlings for those of any draught intermediate between the two main types could be readily derived. This flexibility in its turn allowed, through a redistribution of material, greater simplicity in construction and consequent saving of labour, material and weight. Some old special classes such as spar deck and awning deck were swept away. These complications of design had befogged the matter of classification long enough—even, as will be recalled, involving the Society in litigation.

Another task of revision was undertaken in 1925. This concerned the Rules for the construction of oil tankers, by then being produced in ever-increasing numbers. The specific problems here were those presented by the Isherwood system of longitudinal framing, and during the investigation the Society enjoyed the assistance of Sir Joseph Isherwood himself as well as that of a special sub-committee of builders, owners and designers with intimate experience of ships of this type. Once again, as in the case of the new Rules for Steel Ships, the Society worked out a set of requirements that stood till after the Second World War.

Such revisions, to be sure, were simply adjustments of old statutes to changed conditions, and several other sets of old Rules came up for overhaul during the years following the First World War. In the mid-1920's the use of steel having a higher limit of elasticity than ordinary mild steel was developed and, after elaborate comparative tests had been carried out, standards for this type of metal were incorporated in the Rules. Regulations for the testing of anchors and chain cables were tightened up. Many of these adjustments are of only limited technical interest now, but the involvement of Lloyd's Register in international discussions of the old, nagging problem of load lines belongs to the main body of shipping history.

This important matter had been left in the air since the passing of the Merchant Shipping Act of 1890, and the Committee had continued to make freeboard assignments in its terms—more than 12,000 in about 12 years. In 1903, however, the Germans introduced new regulations of their own, and the Board of Trade was thus prompted to a revived interest in the subject. On the committee of inquiry inevitably appointed to consider the question the Society was strongly represented. After the prolonged labour always associated with official proceedings, the British Freeboard Regulations were amended in 1906. This threw a heavy burden of work on the Society's surveyors. Even so, no international agreement had been reached nor, in spite of many conferences, had it been reached when war broke out in 1914.

It is cutting a long story short to report that the International Load Line Conference did not meet until May, 1930, in London. At this gathering the recommendations made by Great Britain, based largely on the experienced advice of Lloyd's Register, were adopted as a basis of discussion. Full agreement was reached on July 5th, 1930, and Dr. James Montgomerie, the Society's Chief Ship Surveyor, was one of the British delegation that signed the Convention on behalf of H.M. Government.

The Convention altered the rules previously in force by emphasising the proper protection of all deck openings and by introducing, for the first time in British ships, special load lines for timber vessels and for ships carrying liquid cargoes in bulk. The reassignment of freeboards again put a heavy strain on the surveying staff, one considerable group being seconded for the work. This was carried out under the superintendence of Mr. W. Watt, a Principal Surveyor on the Chief Ship Surveyor's staff, one of those dedicated men whose knowledge of a complex subject was extensive, peculiar and of international repute.

One of the major developments of the post-First World War period was the formation of National Committees to carry on the work of

Lloyd's Register in countries abroad. That was so important that it will be dealt with separately in a later chapter.

* * * * *

It would be nearly impossible—and it would certainly be tedious for the general reader—to catalogue all the advances in shipbuilding and engineering practice that were made between the two Great Wars. In everything in these departments, however, Lloyd's Register was inevitably involved, and it is necessary to indicate at least the trends of development.

In the nature of things, the demand of the shipowner was for increased speeds, and not only in the passenger trades. One typical product of the period was the "cargo-passenger liner" that could carry a limited number of passengers at a considerably slower speed than that of the transatlantic "greyhound", but could at the same time carry a solid consignment of goods at a much higher speed than that of the old-fashioned tramp. Intermediate vessels of this class are profitably employed on many oceanic routes to-day, and some of the older shipping companies provide admirable services in ships that, carrying 12 or fewer passengers in no great hurry, also carry cargo at higher than average speeds. The essential difference from the shipping man's point of view is precisely that between the average 12 knots or less of the old-fashioned freighter and the average 15 or 16 knots of the cargo-passenger ship.

As for propelling machinery, the period between the wars saw a sort of race between the turbine and the internal combustion engine of the diesel type. For speed in large vessels of liner dimensions the turbine remained in favour, and when ways and means had been found of interpolating gears between turbine engines and propellers, the shaft horse-power of machinery in large passenger ships became formidable.

In the intermediate ranges of shipping, however, the internal combustion engine, of a variety of types, rapidly replaced the standard steam reciprocating engine. The total tonnage of motorships owned in the world rose from three-quarters of a million in 1919 to nearly 17 million in 1939. In the same period the tonnage of steamships increased by only 4½ million. In 1919 the oil-firing of boilers had been applied to 1½ million tons of shipping, but in 1939 20½ million tons out of a total of 51½ million tons of steamships were using oil. The decline of coal for maritime purposes had started.

Every development of the kind, one improvement tumbling on the heels of another, meant more and more work for the Society's technical experts. For example, the Rules for the construction of water-tube boilers came in for considerable amendment in 1922. The higher temperatures involved in the increasing use of steam at high pressures and of superheated steam called for very anxious consideration of the fitness of materials and scantlings, especially of tubes, to cope with the new conditions. The use of special quality steel of high tensile strength for boiler shell plates was approved by the Committee in 1927.

The most considerable of the problems of the period concerned the shafting suitable for use with oil engines. The Society's experts had long before worked out the proper proportions of the shafting connection between propeller or propellers and the conventional steam engine. The internal combustion engine, however, with its quite different torques and impulses, presented quite another set of problems; and in 1921 the Committee amended the existing Rules for the straight shafting of diesel engines proper. But the motorship continued to increase in size, up to the Italian *Augustus* of 32,650 tons gross, and further revision of the shafting regulations became necessary. These were worked out by specialists under the direction of Mr. H. A. Ruck-Keene and in consultation with the leading manufacturers, and in 1930 the Society approved a new and comprehensive set of Rules that finally imposed order in a new and difficult department of engineering.

The uses of electricity on board ship came to form still another and important field of specialist inquiry, acquiring vast importance as the use of power in this form extended from mere illumination to wireless telegraphy and telephony, gyroscopic compasses and stabilisers, steering gear, direction finders, ventilation, heating, lighting, winches, capstans, cooking, refrigeration, pumps and, finally, propulsion. In any modern ship of size the engine room staff includes a proportion of specialist Electrician Officers.

The electric lighting of ships at sea is an old story now. Kipling's reference to "purrin' dynamoes" in "Macandrew's Hymn" dates from 1893, but installations were at work 14 years before that. It is not quite certain whether the Pacific Steam Navigation Company's *Mendoza* or the Inman liner *City of Berlin* was the first to be fitted with what was invariably called "the electric light". The claim for the *Mendoza* is the better documented. This ship sailed from Liverpool to the Clyde towards the end of 1879, her saloon lit by two electric lights, powered from a Gramme dynamo that had been used in the boiler shop of the builders, Robert Napier & Sons, of Govan. In the course of the voyage the shutters of the saloon were closed and the lights switched on, then switched off for a few minutes to demonstrate the difference between its brilliance and ordinary candle light: no doubt to the accompaniment of much enthusiastic wagging of Victorian beards.

Early in December, 1879, the *City of Berlin* sailed from the Mersey for New York with "the electric light" fitted throughout the passenger deck. The saloon was by now brilliantly lit and, adds a contemporary account, even "the steerage, usually the most gloomy part of the vessel, was lighted up in all parts". The use of electricity on board ship, however, was long confined to lighting, but it was not long before electricity as an illuminant became more than a "tourist attraction" when its increasing use in oil tankers raised that besetting bogey of all men who have to do with ships—fire at sea.

This issue was openly raised in 1890 by an underwriter, Mr. J. Carr Saunders, who acted in that capacity for the Commercial Union Assurance Company and was also a member of the Committee of Lloyd's Register. In a circular letter to interested parties—"with the object of obtaining information respecting methods of installation of the electric light and the use of this light on board vessels"—he invited remarks and suggestions on the subject "so as to eliminate as far as practicable the risk of fire which at present appears to attend the use of the electric light". This appeal, if hardly a model of English prose, stirred the Society to the extent that Dr. Milton, then but recently appointed Chief Engineer Surveyor, was instructed to go into the matter with leading manufacturers of electric lighting equipment, and in 1891 the first set of regulations dealing with the subject was issued, the Committee being careful to say that these were only suggestions.

Three years later, however, some of these requirements were made compulsory, remaining in force with only a few modifications until 1916, when the Institution of Electrical Engineers set up a Special Committee, on which the Society was represented along with Government departments, insurance companies and other interested bodies. The gist of the report and draft regulations of this body were finally embodied in a set of Rules issued by the Society in April, 1920. It is nevertheless hardly possible now to see that the fire alarm sounded by Mr. Saunders in 1890 was quite such a serious matter as appeared at the time. The notation "Elec.Light" was solemnly entered in the Register Book against the names of vessels possessing that sort of equipment, but of the new ships built to the Society's class in 1890 only 51 carried the label. It went right out of use in 1934.

It was a much more serious concern when, the number of motor-ships increasing, shipbuilders took to using electricity to drive auxiliaries that had previously been powered by steam. These appliances used electrical power in substantial quantities—as in steering gear, pumps, winches, refrigeration and heating—and the factor of safety became of renewed importance: all the more so when electric auxiliaries came to be used extensively even in steam vessels. To oversee these new developments the Society decided to appoint as surveyors engineers trained in electricity, and the first two Electrical Engineers joined the staff in 1917, one at Glasgow and the other at Newcastle. Further appointments were made in London and at Liverpool later on. Now the Chief Engineer Surveyor's staff includes a Principal Electrical Engineer supervising a staff of 36 surveyors in this field.

But the day was already approaching when electricity was to be used to drive propelling machinery. The first application of this technique was probably that of John P. Holland in the prototype of the first submarines of the Royal Navy, in 1902. A year later the method was used commercially in the *Wandal*, a ship of 1,150 tons built for use on the Caspian Sea for Nobel's explosives concern and powered by three 120 h.p. direct current motors.

The use of electricity for propulsion has been vastly extended since then, and even the landlubber must have encountered, perhaps with a faint puzzlement, such terms as "turbo-electric" or "diesel-electric". In such cases—and the technique has been applied to ships of considerable size—electric power produced by a turbo-driven or diesel-driven generator is transmitted to a motor directly coupled to the propeller shafting.

Lastly, a special application of electricity, one of increasing importance—the welding of ship's plates under the searing, livid flame of the electrode arc. This was a major revolution in the technique of ship construction.

All those who have lived in, or merely passed through, a busy ship-building town know that the air is filled throughout the working day by the incessant drumming, like distant machine-gun fire, of riveting tools driven by compressed air. Some of us, alas! are old enough to recall how, not so very long ago, ship riveting was a wholly manual job, the mighty hammer and forearms of the riveter smashing against the pressures of his "holder-on" on the other side of the shell, the red-hot bolts dexterously thrown upwards with tongs by the rivet-boy at his stove. Now even the clamour of pneumatic riveting tends to diminish as more and more of the work of binding ships' plates together is done by arc welding and as large sections of any ship can be prefabricated in the sheds and shops.

Obviously, this revolution in basic method profoundly concerned the Society and its experts as indeed it did all concerned with shipping, and there was much shaking of greying heads. Welding would make for a smoother hull, so to speak, and raise the speed of production; but could a hull of welded plates stand up to the fluctuating stresses put upon any floating thing under power in a seaway? The matter was put to the proof by the construction, thanks to the enterprise of Cammell Laird & Company of Birkenhead, of the *Fullagar*. This was a small ship of only 150 feet in length, but welded throughout and not a rivet in her: the work being carried out under the supervision of the Society's surveyors.

The performance of this pioneer craft at sea was closely watched; and the behaviour and sturdiness of the *Fullagar* were proved to the extent that the little ship was cannily classed in Lloyd's Register Book for 1920 as "⨁100A1 Electrically Welded, Subject to Biennial Survey—Experimental". She was perhaps a sporadic phenomenon; years were to pass before the welded ship was fully approved and accepted; but the award of class demonstrated the old Society's alertness in the matter of new developments.

The welding issue illustrates nicely, if obliquely, how the technical advances during the period immediately following the First World War vastly extended the range of the Society's activities. Thus, the welded ship having apparently "arrived", the technicians of Lloyd's Register had immediately to turn their attention to the efficiency of the instruments with which the process of welding is carried out. This gradual spread of interest from the artifact to the raw material out of which it is fashioned has had many interesting applications.

During the second decade of this century the Society's experts are found examining the efficiency of electrodes—the burning points of the welding tools—and a List of Approved Electrodes is published. As we have seen, if steam was to be used at increasingly high pressures and temperatures, then the quality of boiler shell plates had to be examined and certified. If oil was to be used in rapidly increasing quantities, then the conditions of its storage must be investigated for safety's sake.

From the specifically maritime fields, the Society's concern spread to a wide variety of non-marine subjects. As early as 1914 it had undertaken to inspect and test structural steel on behalf of H.M. Office of Works. In much the same department—though it might be described as almost amphibious—the Society supervised much of the work on the materials and machinery for two large floating docks, one to be based at Southampton, the other at Lagos, West Africa. All the complex material for a huge power station at Monte Video was passed under inspection in 1930. Both foreign governments and private firms came to rely on the facilities and high standards of Lloyd's Register for the inspection in quantity of anything from steel rails to canvas hose, from drainage pipes to diving apparatus. The work of the Society's officers on the problems of welding bore fruit in a wide demand for the proper certification of vessels or containers to hold, on land, large quantities of gases or inflammable liquids.

One adventure into the new field of aeronautics should be put on record at least briefly. It was in 1919 that the Committee was approached by the Society of British Aircraft Constructors with the suggestion that Lloyd's Register should undertake the inspection and classification of aircraft on much the same lines as those applicable to ships. Leading underwriters strongly supported the proposal, and officials of the Air Council were interested. The compilation and publication of a Register of Aircraft was actually envisaged.

At the time, however, the aircraft industry did not, to put it bluntly, quite know where it was and where it was going, and it was not until 1927 that new talks were held with Sir Sefton Brancker, then Director of Civil Aviation, and not until 1929 that the Society was encouraged to go ahead. In January, 1930, an Aviation Advisory Committee of Lloyd's Register was established and an Inspector of Civil Aircraft appointed.

This move had enthusiastic backing from many firms and societies connected with the development of flying, Imperial Airways included. Additional aircraft surveyors were appointed, and some engineer surveyors were seconded to gain experience at various airfields and in aircraft factories. The future seemed rosy, and in 1932—a prophetic move, as we shall see—the aircraft departments of Lloyd's Register and of the British Corporation were amalgamated. It was soon perceived, however, that the authority granted to this joint surveying body by the Air Ministry was so limited as to be unacceptable. No doubt in the interests of Defence, the Ministry restricted the right of survey and certification to a narrow group of aircraft privately owned or in the possession of flying clubs; and when the Ministry was approached on the subject in 1933, it took the good old way of setting up a Special Committee to enquire into the working of the existing Air Navigation Regulations, with particular reference to those affecting private flying.

Lord Gorell was the Chairman. In the fullness of time his Special Committee came out with a nice compliment to the Joint Aviation Advisory Committee of Lloyd's Register and the British Corporation, who "have shown generous public spirit in maintaining its work in spite of continuous and heavy losses incurred since its formation". The solid suggestion was that the control of airworthiness for civil aircraft should be delegated to an autonomous Board, Lloyd's Register and the British Corporation to be its effective agents. The rest was silence; and there, as the phrase goes, the matter rested. After a few hesitant years the Society's interest in the subject ended completely.

As the Centenary of the remodelled Society approached, duly to be celebrated at a banquet in the Savoy Hotel in October, 1934, the years had exacted the inevitable toll. Now in the Chair was Sir

George Higgins, C.B.E., who brought to the office some refreshing ideas as to the Society's function and the position of the Chairman himself as the man-on-the-spot. The Deputy-Chairman and Treasurer was Mr. Arthur L. Sturge who, like Sir George Higgins, had held office since 1928. The chairmanship of the Sub-Committee of Classification had meanwhile taken on its proper importance, and that onerous office was held in 1934, and had been since 1923, by Mr. J. Howard Glover.

On the technical side Dr. James Montgomerie was still in the saddle as Chief Ship Surveyor, but Mr. Ruck-Keene had died in 1932 and been succeeded by Dr. Stanley F. Dorey. Most triumphantly of all, Andrew Scott remained Secretary as he had been since 1904. It was in this Centenary year that he was, properly, elevated to the dignity of knighthood. Andrew Scott had been in many respects the *eminence grise* of Lloyd's Register. New attitudes towards the distribution of influence and responsibility within an organisation growing rapidly in authority and scope were, however, to follow his death.

Within such a thoroughly representative body as Lloyd's Register of Shipping the names and distinctions come and go, and the Society goes on. The historian may be allowed to suggest that the happiest circumstance attending the formal celebration of the 1934 Centenary of the reorganised Society was that it nearly coincided with the launch of the *Queen Mary*, that great ship which, with her sister *Queen Elizabeth*, represents the apotheosis of the British genius in shipbuilding. These are not freak ships; their greatness does not lie in their size and speed. It is in their absolute fitness for a given task that they excel.

Hard commercial thinking in Liverpool reached the conclusion that the ideal North Atlantic ferry could best be maintained by two large, fast ships crossing in either direction weekly. The Cunard Company's experts in marine architecture and engineering worked out the basic plans. These were refined by their colleagues in John Brown's shipyard and at the Parsons' works on the Tyne. Lloyd's Register of Shipping lent to this task on the national scale the riches of accumulated wisdom and experience. The rest lay with the craftsmen at Clydebank, heirs to the tradition founded nearly 100 years before by Robert Napier, when he built for Samuel Cunard of Nova Scotia his first four ships of 206 feet in length and 420 horse power. The two

Queens perfectly express those qualities of fitness and soundness that it has been the unresting business of Lloyd's Register of Shipping to establish and maintain.

At the Centenary dinner in the Savoy Hotel the principal guest and speaker was the Right Hon. Walter Runciman, M.P., President of the Board of Trade and a member of a great shipping family. In the course of his speech he said:—

> ". . . You have classified more ships than all the other Classification Societies in the world put together for many long years. You have done so on an international basis, which has given uniformity to the trades you serve so well . . . You have standardised everything that is best in material and design, and . . . you have made a contribution to the safety of travel which could not have been made by any other means."

The Report for that year announced that more than 95 per cent of the total tonnage being built in Great Britain and Ireland, and fully 75 per cent of the total under construction throughout the world, was under the Society's survey for classification.

CHAPTER 11   NATIONAL SERVICE AGAIN

THE Centenary celebrations of 1934 took place at a time when the world was only starting to emerge from the depression that had broken upon the United States in 1929. That nearly parallel episode, the launch of the *Queen Mary* at Clydebank, was no more than the beginning of the end of a long period of frustration and unemployment, during which the huge hull had lain for more than a year on the stocks, an empty, soundless shell, while—as newspaper reports kept assuring us—starlings and magpies nested in the gantries. They were a little less accurate in informing us that the unfinished ship was "rusting" in idleness—as if the Cunard White Star Company, shipbuilders with the experience of Messrs. John Brown & Company, the surveyors of Lloyd's Register, not to mention the underwriters involved, would be inclined to spare a lick of paint and coats of linseed oil for the preservation of a hull worth millions of pounds.

The Annual Reports of Lloyd's Register of Shipping are always admirable mirrors of the trends of world trade, and throughout the fourth decade of the 20th Century their tone was far from ebullient. The consequences of the depression are now seen to have been commercially more serious than those arising directly out of the First World War. During the 12 months ended June 30th, 1934, the Society's classification was assigned to only 192 ships of 350,430 tons gross—as compared with 4,250,000 tons in 1919–20! Of the meagre 1934 total only 136,072 tons were constructed in Great Britain and Ireland. Production increased between 1935 and 1937, but the vagaries of freight rates, higher wages and advancing costs of material so slowed down production that the last Annual Report to be published before the outbreak of the Second World War in 1939 recorded another melancholy drop in tonnage under construction.

In the Annual Reports of the period, indeed, the note of anxiety is hardly ever absent. They remind us that one of the problems of that phase was the disposal of redundant and/or obsolescent tonnage. It is perhaps well we should be reminded of the innumerable ships that swung idly at anchor in almost every estuary of the British Isles—the worn-out tramps, the shabby "Standard" ships of the period of emergency, even the liners that, the darlings of their day, had long outlived it.

The relative instability of the period, however, did not by any means slacken the strain on the Society and its experts. Indeed, the tentative and experimental character of technical progress during these years was a perpetual challenge. Oil firing, welding, electric propulsion, the special stresses set up by new applications of power, the refinement of metals—these and a dozen other considerations required closer attention than ever.

The senior technical officers of Lloyd's Register were called upon to travel more and more widely, often as members of official commissions, more often both to give and seek advice on the latest advances; for it was distinctly an age in which frontiers within the scientific world were being broken down. The new problems of refrigeration and other recondite issues were investigated and discussed. We find the Society responsible in 1929 for the survey and classification of the *Vikingen*, one of the earliest of those strange monsters of the deep—a floating whale oil factory of 20,000 tons. A succession of failures in steering gears of the rod-and-chain type led to a tightening of the survey regulations. Welding had come to stay, as the phrase goes; and the different types of electrodes approved by Lloyd's Register were now counted in hundreds.

The most marked feature of the period in the department of shipping, however, was the ever-increasing use of heavy oil engines. Several firms on the Continent had perfected their own improvements or adaptations of the system, to the extent that in the early 1920's the Society appointed one of its engineer surveyors for permanent duty at the Sulzer works in Switzerland. Several leading shipbuilding firms in Great Britain arranged to build under licence their own engines according to one or other of these patents; and during the uneasy 1930's the number of ships built to be driven by oil engines greatly exceeded that of those using turbines, and began to exceed that of those using the old, standard reciprocating steam engines.

Just a few figures from the Annual Report of Lloyd's Register for 1937–38, the last to be published before the outbreak of the Second World War, tell the tale clearly. The figures are given here in the round.

Of almost exactly 1,500,000 of tonnage classed, 433,000 relied on steam reciprocating engines, 192,000 on steam turbines, and 878,000 on internal combustion engines—the last two figures including turbo-electric or diesel-electric installations. As for fuel, this great mass of shipping relied on coal to the tune of 19·4 per cent and on oil to the extent of 80·6 per cent. Of the 1,011 ships launched in 1937 reciprocating engines were installed in 374, turbines in 55 and diesels in 582.

The increasing emphasis on oil had its obvious effects on the work of the Society and its surveyors. Tankers for the carriage of oil across the seas increased in number and size, and the system of "Arcform" construction for such great ships, patented by the resourceful Sir Joseph Isherwood, required special study, even if it was never adopted to any notable extent. The general trend naturally heightened the concern of the large oil companies for the strength and safety of pressure vessels and other plant which, of ever increasing capacity, were being installed in oil fields and refineries.

The Anglo-Iranian Oil Company (now the British Petroleum Company) and also, later, the Iraq Petroleum Company turned to the

I

Society for advice as to the inspection of their plant and equipment in the Middle East. In September, 1936, Dr. S. F. Dorey, the Society's Chief Engineer Surveyor, and a member of his staff visited Abadan to advise on safety inspection methods. A year later the Society undertook the control of the Company's Plant Survey Department in Abadan and retained this control until the nationalisation of the refinery in 1951, when British personnel were compelled to withdraw. A similar service was provided for the Iraq Petroleum Company in Kirkuk.

The extension of the Society's work in non-marine directions took several forms. Bridge-building steel was tested in large quantities, and much structural steel for H.M. Office of Works was inspected. The increase in the number of refrigerated ships was reflected in a vast enlargement of refrigerated storage capacity ashore, and millions of cubic feet of such accommodation required inspection and approval.

It is a fair assumption now that much of the material tested for the Office of Works went into the establishments being set up during the late 1930's, perhaps belatedly, under the heading of Defence. The Annual Report of Lloyd's Register, however, eschews political references. Even the Minutes of the General Committee only occasionally reflect the anxieties that plagued its members, all well-informed and responsible men.

On September 29th, 1938, "the Chairman referred to the fact that, in view of the international situation, it might be necessary for decisions to be taken at a moment's notice; and it was AGREED THAT any urgent matters arising could safely be left to be dealt with by the Three Chairs"—that is, by the Chairman of the General Committee, the Deputy Chairman and Treasurer and the Chairman of the Sub-Committees of Classification.

This was the Munich period. Readers of the older generation will recall that it coincided with the launch of the *Queen Elizabeth* at Clydebank, that King George the Sixth could not leave London, and that the ceremony was conducted by the lady who is now the Queen Mother. In June, 1939—having approved a substantial subscription to the *Thetis* disaster fund—the Committee made provision to convert at a cost of £1,000 the basement of a nearby warehouse as an air raid shelter for the 160 workers in the Printing House in Southwark. In August of that fateful year the Chairman was authorised to negotiate the purchase of a property called High Close, at Wokingham, Berkshire, described as being "in a reception area".

* * * * *

So darkness fell on September 3rd, 1939, and the affairs of Lloyd's Register of Shipping slipped into the blackout of Security. The records of the Society's work during the Second World War are less easily available than those applying to the 1914–18 period, for the simple reason that the organisation was between 1939 and 1945 more fully absorbed in the machinery of National Defence and more completely at the disposal of Government Departments, notably the Admiralty and the Ministry of Transport.

So the report on these proceedings must be largely negative. The Register Book was duly corrected and printed throughout the war years, but it was a "secret" document and its circulation was rigorously restricted. No Annual Report was issued in printed form between 1938 and 1950. The strain on the surveying staff was fantastically heavy, but not more so than that on the higher management of the Society. It is on record that the sections of the administrative staff, evacuated to Wokingham, got through rather more work than they were wont to do in London, simply because they were relieved of the strain of travelling to and from suburban homes through the blackout in London and were happy to put in extra hours during the evenings in the country. For a considerable period during the war the Chief Ship Surveyor and the staff concerned with plans worked from the Glasgow office, and some other sections were "decentralised" and distributed among the larger shipbuilding regions. Otherwise, the senior men on the technical side and the secretarial staff remained in London.

The office escaped serious damage by direct hit during the air raids, but the firewatchers admirably performed their wearing and dangerous duties. Undoubtedly the strangest feature of the emergency was the unprecedented authority and volume of work imposed on the Chairmen, Sir George Higgins until 1943 and Mr. Ernest Lionel Jacobs thereafter. In a sense, with the help of only a skeleton staff; with the Committee meeting only occasionally and all manner of decisions having to be taken at short notice, the Chairmen and their Deputy, Sir Ronald Garrett, were thrust into a position of virtual dictatorship and forced to work longer hours in the interest of the Society alone than many of their predecessors would have found tolerable.

These difficulties were aggravated by the incidence of what would otherwise have been normal changes within the staff. During the middle period of the war the office of Secretary changed hands more than once; and until Mr. Percy E. Clement was provisionally appointed in 1943 the Chairman and Deputy-Chairmen had to assume many of the responsibilities. There then arose the case of the retirement of Dr. James Montgomerie from the high position of Chief Ship Surveyor, which he had continued to fill well beyond the normal age of retirement. Fortunately, the Society was able to secure from the Admiralty the release of Mr. R. B. Shepheard, who had served Lloyd's Register well in Germany and then in the United States and had been seconded to Whitehall as a specialist in welding.

In 1946, when it was all over at last, the Chairman addressed the General Committee of Lloyd's Register on the Society's vicissitudes during the war years. Mr. Jacobs commanded a racy style of speech and was no great respecter of either persons or institutions. This address was never reported, but it is now permissible to quote a few passages from a heartfelt oration. It started handsomely:—

> "I wish to dedicate this talk to our Staff, who have put in some wonderful work during the war period . . . I like to feel that I have to a certain extent shared in their work during the whole time. For long periods we did not have the benefit of the Committee's advice, and it is pleasant to be able to feel that we carried on without any unpleasant denouements. Difficulties there were—many of them— but they were overcome; and I should like to say that, while at moments I hated all Ministries, it must be heartily admitted that the official world was most helpful."

Mr. Jacobs went on to say something about the increasing strain put upon the Chairman and Deputy-Chairman, observing:—

> "We are, of course, mainly concerned with 'policy' decisions, and in these days you will realise they are many and varied. Just as a small instance, I find that at present the appointment of a Surveyor to a foreign port is not just the naming of an able technical man,

but political considerations have also to be thought of, with resultant necessary contacts and correspondence. In other words, in these present unsettled times, the Chairmanship is a whole time job."

That speech was prophetic in adumbrating certain attitudes the Society was obliged to adopt in a changing world, notably the realisation that the Chairmanship of the Committee of Lloyd's Register could no longer be taken as a nice compliment to a veteran shipping man who would look in for a couple of hours on the mornings of four or five days a week; also that the new patterns of nationalism were to present new problems to an institution that had only international good as its largest objective.

*   *   *   *   *

Mr. Jacobs's speech was delivered behind closed doors, but at the same time there was issued to the Press a summary of the work done by Lloyd's Register and its overworked surveyors during the period of hostilities. To a considerable extent the experience of the First World War was repeated, but during the Second the authority of the Admiralty and the Ministry of Transport was much more comprehensive. Both these Departments required their own surveying staffs to be largely augmented, and Lloyd's Register was hard put to it at once to supply these reinforcements and keep its own services going.

With regard to merchant shipbuilding, the Government's programme provided that each builder should concentrate on the type of vessel with which he and his workers had been most familiar in times of peace. This was a sensible step, leading to a reduction in the number of types to be produced, and it was the Society's business to examine and approve the different structural plans. The vast majority of merchant vessels produced under this emergency programme were therefore built to the classification of Lloyd's Register; while, at the same time, the surveyors had to supervise construction of tonnage built to special Government requirements. In all, during the war years, 5,500,000 tons of new ships were classed in the U.K. alone—an astonishing feat in the face of the blackout, air-raids, travelling difficulties and so on.

Since the United States were involved in the war at a relatively

117

early stage of the proceedings, the Society was not so heavily engaged on that side of the Atlantic as it had been in the 1914–1918 period, but before the picture changed with the assault on Pearl Harbour a Government Mission went to the States, in September, 1940, to arrange for construction of merchant ships in American yards. Of this body the Society's Principal Surveyor for the United States and Canada and the Principal Engineer Surveyor in New York were members.

The Mission quickly succeeded in having two shipyards specially laid out to meet the British need for merchant shipping: one at Portland, Maine, the other at Richmond, California; and contracts were placed for 60 ships of the "Ocean" type. These, practically all-welded, were built to the Society's classification, and once again a number of the dwindling force of experienced surveyors had to be sent out from Britain to supervise the jobs. After Pearl Harbour the United States Maritime Commission took over the work, and the yards at Portland and Richmond and elsewhere turned with charac-teristic vigour to the mass-production of those "Liberty" and other types that made such a large contribution to the ultimate victory. The American genius for bold, large-scale production was of critical influence in the long run, but the British contribution, through Lloyd's Register, of precise standards as expressed in the prototype "Ocean" class, must come high in the reckoning of credit.

This massive drive in North America had one effect that has not been fully appreciated in Britain to this day. This was the emergence of the Dominion of Canada as a shipbuilding power. In one way of putting it, the Canadians had the advantage of the American example in mass production and of the British insistence on high standards of construction. They had very limited shipbuilding resources to begin with, but they came into the business with a right good will.

This was at a time when the Americans produced a Liberty ship in 85 days on the average—35 days for fabrication and sub-assembly, 40 days on the ways, and 10 days in outfitting. Some remarkable records, however, were set up. For example, one Liberty ship was launched at Oregon Yard ten days after the keel had been laid; and Richmond No. 2 retorted by assembling a ship in only four days on the ways! These special efforts—or sporting events—called for elaborate feats of pre-assembly, and special concentration on organisation and the use of manpower, cranes and so on. Probably the fastest rate at which construction could have been maintained was 17 days on the ways—that is, between keel-laying and launching.

These extraordinary feats presented the Canadians with a challenge, and this was brilliantly met. Though much of the labour available had to learn as it worked, Canada produced during those years of strain in the way of cargo ships, tankers, corvettes, frigates, transport ferries, minesweepers and other craft more than 500 ships of some 2,250,000 gross tons: an astounding performance from the technical as well as from the patriotic point of view.

Inevitably, the staff of surveyors in Canada had to be greatly increased to deal with this output. Some of these were drawn from the States after the U.S. Maritime Commission had taken over in that country, but still more had to be spared from the dwindling pool at home. The strain was cruelly persistent. During the emergency Australia made her contribution according to her resources. There were created at Whyalla in South Australia, on the edge of semi-desert country, a shipyard and a harbour; and out of this remote establishment as well as from Australia's already existing resources came a useful contribution to Allied shipping strength, especially in the Pacific. Once more the onus of supervision fell on the patient surveyors of Lloyd's Register.

At home, as has been noted, the burden of the Society's responsibilities was preponderantly in the department of merchant shipping; in addition, as had happened during the First World War, its experts were called upon to inspect and test enormous quantities of shell steel—up to 18,000 tons a week at the peak and nearly 3,000,000 tons in all. When the time came, all the high tensile steel for the Bailey Bridges that so greatly eased the advances of Allied armies was inspected and tested in the same way, and it was the surveyors' special concern to make sure that all the bars should be dead straight, all surfaces flat and all sections exactly square to each other: each section, as in an expensive toy, ready to be fitted into the whole within closely defined limits.

The tale of participation in the war effort is endless—a hand in the enterprise code-named "Pluto", the pipeline laid across the Channel to feed the invading armies with oil; the inspection of power plant and equipment for the relief of Russia and other devastated regions;

a surveyor lent to the Ministry of Food to be Director of Cold Stores, and all machinery for the new cold stores put up by the Government inspected by the Society's men . . . even surveyors to follow the advancing Allied Armies and be on hand to give help as required in the liberated countries.

Two concerns more nearly along the normal lines of Lloyd's Register business were of special interest.

For the propulsion of tank landing craft a large number of oil engines of the 12-cylinder Paxman-Ricardo type were required, and the assembly of these units presented a heartbreaking problem. It was solved by ordering the constituent parts from more than 300 sub-contractors, by whom they were forwarded to two erecting centres to be assembled and then tested. All the work of supervising the assembly fell on the Society's surveyors who, when the war ended, had overseen the completion of some 3,500 engines of this type.

At the same time, inevitably, the Royal Navy was crying out for auxiliary craft of all kinds, and some 2,000 ships in this wide category, large and small but aggregating well over 1,000,000 gross tons, were built under the Society's supervision. This service required the posting of a representative of Lloyd's Register to Admiralty headquarters at Bath as Liaison Officer, but it involved also an industrious scraping of the barrel to discover even the most modest reserves of building power. This had an almost romantic sequel in the creation of the Fairmile Marine Company.

The Fairmile concern simply roped in almost every small boatyard, yacht and repair slip along the coasts, creeks and canals of the British Isles and set them to work *in wood*, that tractable material which had been almost the only material known to the Lloyd's surveyors of nearly 200 years before. A more sophisticated expert, but still a Lloyd's Register surveyor, was lent to the Company as a Special Surveyor for Wood Construction, and he was appointed its Production Manager in due course. One may imagine that this officer found a vast deal of interest and variety in his work, breathing new life into an ancient craft; and he certainly contrived to produce out of an old hat and under the Society's survey some 700 wood motor launches, motor gunboats and motor torpedo boats.

There was other work in wood to be supervised for the Admiralty, notably the building of 281 motor minesweepers outwith the Fairmile programme, but these respectable figures are seen to be trivial as compared with those for construction in steel. It had been perceived by the Admiralty before the outbreak of war that the services of the Classification Societies would have to be enlisted to augment its own inspection services, and it was conceded that, so far as auxiliary craft might be concerned, the standards applicable to merchant ships would suffice in a period of rapid production quite as adequately as the more austere requirements of naval practice. When the hour struck, no written contract or specific instructions were exchanged. Lloyd's Register of Shipping embarked on its task as a sort of free agent of Admiralty in the auxiliary field.

During the war the naval auxiliary vessels built to the Society's classification included 93 minesweepers of the Bangor and Algerine classes; 174 anti-submarine, minesweeping trawlers; 91 corvettes of the Flower and Castle classes, and 87 frigates of the River and Loch classes, along with scores of tugs, salvage vessels, mooring vessels, barges, lighters and such.

The largest effort, however, was in the direction of producing landing craft. This was first inspired by a military setback, when the Prime Minister was appalled by the Navy's lack of large craft for carrying assault tanks. The keels of three heavy tank landing ships, *Boxer*, *Bruiser* and *Thruster*, were promptly laid, these always to be known, affectionately if a little facetiously, as "Winettes" in honour of the bold spirit who had ordained their creation. However, as the prospect of invading the Continent grew nearer, it was seen that the operations would require large fleets of small ships for landing tanks and troops on enemy-held beaches. The effort in this direction of the Society and its experts is among the great, unsung records of war achievement.

The first yards for prefabricating and assembling these ships were laid down on the Tees, with one of the Society's surveyors in charge. Wonders were worked on Tees-side, and the programme was extended to several other parts of the Kingdom at which suitable building sites, materials and labour, largely female, were available. In all, 420 landing craft of this class were built to the Society's requirements, while many others were fabricated under the Society's supervision but put together under direct Admiralty supervision.

During the war period the Society classed a total of 2,139 auxiliary vessels within the United Kingdom and 241 in Canada—the latter figure including 70 invaluable frigates and 52 corvettes. To phrase it very modestly, the Admiralty and the Allied cause were well served in the emergency by a civilian organisation.

But that was not the whole tale of improvisation during those years of war; the Society's almost puritanical concern for high standards had to absorb many shocks during the period of hostilities. There had to be, by the Act of God and those of the King's Enemies, a slackening of the Rules governing the periodical survey of classed ships, but the most desperate problems presented to the surveying staff during the direst period of the emergency had to do with the repair of ships damaged by enemy action.

Even the layman can easily appreciate the agonised nature of the questions posed by any vessel that has encountered a torpedo or a stick of bombs, perhaps with her bows and foc'sle shot off, her stern and steering gear a mess. Could the damage be repaired with a reasonable prospect of the ship's survival on going to sea again? If so, what shipyard, already cluttered with the construction of new tonnage, could undertake the job? Why not write the vessel off as a hopeless case, every job costing hundreds of thousands of pounds of the country's diminishing resources?

Wholesale damage to shipping and the relative infrequency of thorough surveys during the war years left the Society with a host of outstanding problems after V-J Day, and there will be something to say about these later on. Despite all the alarms and crises of the period, however, the Minutes of the General Committee reflect only the calm of an ancient and experienced institution going about its business in the usual way. So far from closing down, the Research branch went on working calmly, preparing the ground for new rules, for example, in the realms of electric welding, reduction gear design and manufacture, and torsional vibration in diesel engine crankshafts and propeller shafts. Before the war ended the Committee approved schemes whereby X-ray inspection would be applied to welded seams in ship plates and in pressure vessels for boilers, etc.

Just two small entries on the human side seem to carry a reassurance that the world was not quite utterly mad during those years.

In June, 1943, the Ministry of Transport intimated that it wished to make a payment of 100 guineas to a surveyor of the Society who had rendered it services of outstanding value. The reply was that, while the gesture was appreciated, the payment of a grant of this nature would be contrary to the Committee's practice. And then—the Society's independence thus vindicated, the Minute concludes:—

> "ORDERED
> That the question of the Society making a grant to Mr. M——
> be left to the Chairman and Deputy-Chairman to decide."

Then, in September, 1944, there came before the Committee the curious and touching case of Miss Bessie Boolds. This lady was the daughter of a former Principal Surveyor at Newcastle and had been left so poorly off that, in 1932, she and her sister had been granted an allowance of 30/- per week from the Stevens Fund, a charitable trust administered by the Committee. Then, on her death, it was reported to the Committee that she had bequeathed the sum of £40 to Lloyd's Register. This modest bequest was turned back into the Fund, of course, but it probably represented the bulk of the poor lady's savings, and it is surely a most touching example of gratitude coming towards the end of a war in which so many of the old decencies seem to have perished.

Mr. Jacobs did well to dedicate his 1946 Report to the Staff. Many of them had worked in dirty and dangerous circumstances; all had been grossly overworked in devoted service to the country in time of grievous emergency. Of those members of staff who joined the Forces seven did not return.

CHAPTER 12   RESTORING THE POSITION

IT was not until 1950 that the Society resumed publication of the Annual Report. One of the Chairmen of the war period, no doubt sharing Lord Randolph Churchill's allergy to "damned dots", went so far indeed as to express the view that there were too many figures and tables of figures in the conventional summary.

Ignoring this unusual opinion, the resuscitated Annual Report for 1949–50 made special reference to tables in an opening statement of much interest, thus:—

> "If the years immediately following World War I were marked by easy optimism, those following World War II have been marked by realism in shipping circles. Difficulties have not been ignored, but faced and often overcome. The replacement of lost tonnage and the rebuilding of the world merchant fleet have not been deterred

by unrest and uncertainty, but rather the reverse, and the 31,000 steamers and motorships which constitute the 84·6 million ton world fleet of 1950 are a far more efficient instrument of commerce than the 30,000 ships which made up the 68·5 million ton fleet of 1939 . . .

"Apart from the increase in average size of ships and in economy of operation, the most notable change has been in distribution. The German, Italian and Japanese merchant fleets are only a fraction of their former size, and the United States of America now has the highest total tonnage registered under one flag, although a considerable part of it is in reserve, and Britain has by far the largest merchant fleet in active employment.

"To meet the new position, naval architects and marine engine designers have been stimulated to fresh efforts in the production of more efficient ships. In this the Society's experience has frequently been of great service, and a constant endeavour is made to keep the constructional Rules abreast of developments; at a time when new methods and materials are being employed to counter rising costs, it is particularly important to ensure that their use involves no sacrifice of durability and ease of maintenance in the finished product."

The orderly approach to normality in the Society's technical concerns was reflected in a new approach to relations with the Staff. Salaries, wages and bonuses were continually being adjusted, as of course they were in every branch of industry. The Society had to take into account the serious problems of housing in the larger outports as well as in London and to provide for assistance in house purchase by employees. In the special nature of its scope, it had to deal with many tricky questions arising out of the position of officers who had suffered through enemy action. One domestic feature of the period—seeming quite comically "dated" 14 years later—is memorialised in a solemn Minute of Committee for March 14th, 1946:—

"The Chairman mentioned that it was contemplated to continue the employment of ladies on the staff in the London Office. These have so far been engaged on a temporary basis, but it was felt the time had now arrived when the position should be consolidated by informing some of them that they would be considered as the nucleus of the future female staff."

In the all-important departments of ship construction and marine engineering, the technicians were not called upon to deal with such seismic changes as the substitution of iron for wood in building and

125

oil for coal in propulsion. So far as the general reader need be concerned in these esoteric affairs, the research and surveying staffs were largely involved in (*a*) the development of established techniques and new applications thereof, and (*b*) the correction of weaknesses revealed in the rough-and-tumble of war service.

For example, to take the latter issue first, the all-welded ship had revealed in service certain weaknesses: notably a tendency towards corrugation of the bottom. Why? That was precisely the sort of problem towards which the specialists of Lloyd's Register addressed themselves.

Specific problems in the same general class included that of corrosion in oil tanks and boiler smoke tubes, those associated with the carriage of edible oils in deep tanks, and those arising out of the refrigeration of fish at abnormally low temperatures. In another post-war year we find the specialists watching experiments in the use of the gas turbine for marine propulsion. These, however, were developments in the ordinary run of things, even if the use of the gas turbine seemed as exciting potentially as that of atomic energy has come to be in 1960.

Britain's great fleet of passenger liners was being renewed, but there were to be at that stage no more in the *Queen Mary* class. The Cunard Company itself, the Peninsular & Oriental, the British India, the Union-Castle and other leaders in that trade were content to build elegant but more or less conventional ships of up to 45,000 tons gross but no more, driven at 20 knots or a little more by turbine engines and twin screws.

During the years 1954 and 1955, in fact, the Society and its technical advisers were obliged to consider in the light of changing circumstances a far-reaching reappraisal of the various Construction Rules. A special panel under the Technical Committee went into a variety of new problems, most of these arising out of the fact that ships were, to put it simply, becoming longer, finer in form, with longer machinery spaces amidships and the weight of cargo disposed towards the ends of the vessel. Ships were also running at higher speeds, and that, over and above the elongation of hulls, involved serious considerations of safety. These considerations led the Society to tighten up many rules bearing on the special problems of longitudinal framing and, in consequence, on the desirable weights of scantlings, on efficiency in welding processes, and on the ideal qualities of steel to be used in these new shipbuilding processes.

In the purely marine field the most dramatic feature was the increase in the average size of the oil tanker. The Annual Report of Lloyd's Register of Shipping for 1949–1950 gravely reported on that situation, thus:—

> "Due to a variety of causes, there has been a steady increase in the average size of ships, but the increase in the size of oil tankers is perhaps the most important. The standard 12,000 tons deadweight tanker common before the war has been replaced by a 16,000 to 18,000 tons deadweight class, and still larger ships have been constructed in considerable numbers in this country and abroad. These latter fall mainly into two groups— the 24,000 tons deadweight, having a length of about 560 feet, and the 28,000 tons deadweight, having a length of 600 feet—but tankers of 30,000 tons deadweight are also under construction and even larger capacities are contemplated."

The prophecy, if fairly easy to make, has been justified within 10 years. As we have all come to realise by only too painful processes, the extraction, transport and storage of oil in and from the wells of the Middle East are vital within the economy of Western Europe, and the tanker is running in size up to that of the great ocean liner. The major oil companies have thus become shipowners, looking to Lloyd's Register for the proper classification of their vessels, and this connection led after the Second World War, when Dr. Stanley F. Dorey was Chief Engineer Surveyor, to a large, even rapid expansion of the Society's Non-Marine branch under a Principal Engineer Surveyor.

"Non-Marine" is to some extent a misleading term. This branch has always been closely integrated with the marine survey establishment. Except in just a few cases of specialist surveyors, the marine engineer surveyor can and does work in both fields. The value of this arrangement lies in the fact that it allows the technical staff to broaden its experience of engineering advances. For example, the Society's technicians have been much engaged in the inspection of nuclear power stations, and this during the period that has seen the application of nuclear power in sea-going vessels, if only in submarines in the first place.

The term Non-Marine was dropped in 1956, when the department was reconstituted as the Land Division under a Sub-Committee of the

General Committee. Its work has continued to increase, especially in connection with atomic energy contracts, all manner of components in these vast schemes requiring examination of the most searching kind. It has supervised site contracts in the Middle East and Australia and a distillation plant in Kuwait; inspected huge hydro-electric schemes in Australia, Canada and South Africa—indeed, in almost every Commonwealth country, and in Turkey as well. It has taken in the inspection of plant and equipment for oil refineries from Grangemouth to Baghdad by way of Cartagena. The work is now so extensive in scope that senior surveyors have been appointed to co-ordinate the Society's many commitments in many parts of the world. Indeed, the growing importance of this department was specially recognised quite recently when it moved into special headquarters of its own at Croydon.

Highly skilled work of the kind demands research and, again during Dr. Dorey's fruitful period of office, the Research branch was created, now with a laboratory at Crawley and all the necessary apparatus for metallurgical work in particular. The main concern is with metals and their behaviour under various conditions of service, but there is no end to the problems with which the experts may be confronted at any moment. The Society's research surveyors have carried out investigations in many fields often involving problems of vibration, some so complex in character that they have required the use of the most modern types of electronic equipment.

The work of this branch was extended during 1956–57 by the creation of the Engineering Investigation Department, a mobile team of engineer surveyors. Some crisis within the machinery of a considerable ship may at any moment take a clutch of specialists post-haste, usually by air, to far distant parts of the world—South Africa, Java, Western Canada, South America: anywhere. In general, the troubles investigated arise mainly out of the unforeseen stresses in advanced applications of power. Two examples are enough. The first was a successful investigation of gearing failures on several large tankers that had not been classed with Lloyd's Register in the first place. The second was an inquiry into severe axial vibration of shafting in two large turbine-driven cargo liners. The cure recommended was that the propeller should be re-designed, and this had actually the effect of increasing the speed of the ships as well as that of eliminating the vibration completely.

The Society's experts in such esoteric affairs have been involved in some slightly eccentric enterprises. At the outbreak of the Second World War, for example, the authorities were naturally concerned to secure large supplies of canvas hoses for the purposes of Civil Defence. This commodity is, or was, mainly a French product, and surveyors of Lloyd's Register worked on the other side of the Channel, examining and passing 2,000,000 feet of this material until the invasion of the Low Countries brought the work to a halt.

During the middle years of the war, again, the authorities were disturbed by reports that the Germans in North Africa were refrigerating tanks for the comfort and efficiency of their troops, and the Ministry of Supply set up a committee of enquiry, on which Dr. Dorey and members of the Research Department represented the Society. They worked on the larger tank testing grounds; they were given a Valentine tank to play with, and they crawled in and out of it in near-tropical conditions within a laboratory. It was concluded at length that the refrigeration of tanks, already overloaded with gadgets, was not feasible, but the Society's men were able to make recommendations that abated the discomfort of the British soldier in the desert.

Dr. Stanley F. Dorey was an outstanding member of the Society's technical staff. His engineering apprenticeship was served in the Royal Dockyard at Chatham, and he served in the Royal Navy before joining Lloyd's Register as a surveyor in 1919. He rose to become Chief Engineer Surveyor in 1933 and decorated that office for nearly a quarter of a century. Honours came to him copiously; he was at one time or another President of four of the most important technical Institutes, for two years Chairman of Council of the Institution of Naval Architects. Elected a Fellow of the Royal Society in 1948, he became a member of the Council of that austere body. Government Departments sought his advice; he read many papers, many of them bringing him fresh honours, before technical bodies.

Dr. Dorey would certainly have approved the setting-up in the late 1950's of a system of indexing technical reports by the use of cards with punched edges. In the nature of things, the amount of specialised information acquired by the Society's technical staffs over many years was enormous, but since it existed in vast accumulations of hand-written or typewritten documents, the mass became unmanageable and research into it a tedious penance. During the late 1950's the

Paramount card system of indexing was gradually introduced, first for recording only defects in ships' hulls and then for recording machinery defects as well. The inevitable fusion of these branches led to the creation of the Technical Records Branch wherein—though this is to put it crudely—the record cards bearing on the condition of a given ship or on the aspects of a special problem can be so arranged through a simple manipulation of the punched holes that the investigator is presented with a *précis* of the information he seeks.

*　　*　　*　　*　　*

Changes in the technical regions within the scope of Lloyd's Register of Shipping are as inevitable as they are frequent. As the historian sees these things, however, the changes in the administrative and representational character of the Society during the five years that followed V-J Day were quite remarkable within an institution so venerable and fixed in its ways. The solemn decision of the Committee to allow women to regard themselves as permanent members of the staff was only a first stirring of a breeze about the skirts of the "Lady" depicted in the traditional badge.

It has been seen that at least one Chairman in time of war had, thanks in part to shortage of staff, ceased to regard his function as an elegant part-time occupation for a person distinguished in the shipping world and had accepted nearly full-time responsibility for and immediate control of the complex organisation. Another Chairman remarked that the imposing Sir Andrew Scott, the Secretary for so many years, "*was* the Society". Scott's retirement in 1935 and the new determination of later Chairmen to take a larger hand in the day-to-day running of business hastened a process of domestic devolution and a wider distribution of responsibilities that were perhaps overdue.

After the Second War, however, the Society turned to the serious consideration of its general structure, and that in several important aspects. The Chief Ship Surveyor, for example, advised the General Committee that the time had come to revise the Rules for Steel Ships. These Rules are continually changed as a new modification seems desirable, an old regulation found to be no longer applicable in practice. The formal revision from time to time is obviously desirable, perhaps especially for the guidance of officers at the outports, and the post-war revision, the first for nearly a quarter of a century, was certainly overdue. Two other lines of enquiry resulted in constitutional changes of moment.

One of these concerned the composition of the important Technical Committee. As we have seen, this was originally a sub-committee formed in 1890 to allow shipbuilders and engineers, along with representatives of certain technical bodies, a larger say in those conclusions of the Society that affected them, but without representation on the General Committee. A sub-committee headed by Mr. Charles Connell was therefore appointed to look into the position in the light of changed circumstances, and its recommendations were duly accepted in 1948.

By these the representational scope of the Technical Committee was considerably expanded, and not in the United Kingdom alone. The National Committees abroad were invited to appoint delegates, and in the first year of its working representatives from Holland, Denmark, Sweden and Spain attended meetings. The most valuable feature of the reform, however, was the appointment within the Technical Committee of Specialist Panels that can be convened more quickly and get down to business more promptly and at less expense than can the full Committee of 65 members. The prompt report of these specialised recommendations to the General Committee has, within the past 12 years, meant a vast saving of expense and administrative work.

More important still, on December 11th, 1947, the General Committee appointed an *ad hoc* Sub-Committee "to consider the question of revising the Rules relating to the superintendence of the Society". This charmingly archaic phrase adumbrated a wholesale revision of representation on the governing body: in a sense, raising once more all those nice questions that had provoked real bad feeling in earlier days. Underwriters, shipowners, merchants; shipbuilders and engineers; the rebellious outports of the North . . . The makings of a new battle seemed to be there, but tempers were more equable now. It had been seen that Lloyd's Register of Shipping was a national institution of high value and beyond prejudice, and if the old lady was in the mood for spring cleaning, there was nobody to be angry about it, especially since—as will be seen in a moment—a large event in the history of classification was taking place.

131

The recommendations ultimately adopted increased the number of the General Committee by 13 members and considerably altered the balance as between the professional groups represented in the old Society. For example, the Merchant who had been so important in its earlier years disappeared, while the Shipowner was granted a larger proportional representation. The Sub-Committee had carefully considered the fluctuations in trade at the outports, and a few were, so to speak, down-graded and others up-graded. Thus the representations of Cardiff, Leith and Tyne were increased and those of Sunderland and the Hartlepools reduced. The Glasgow Committee of eight members became the Scottish Committee, with 10 members on the General Committee. This number was increased to 15 when the fusion with the British Corporation ultimately took place. An old rule had allowed the General Committee to co-opt up to 12 Shipbuilders and/or Engineers; it was now empowered to bring in additional members not exceeding 12 in number.

There was nothing sensational in these changes. They were necessary and perhaps overdue adjustments to new conditions and an altered balance of influence within the British shipping industry. The new regulations had also the effect of creating a revised framework of responsibility at the highest level. It was decided that there should always be at hand two Deputy-Chairmen: one to be Deputy-Chairman and Treasurer, the other Deputy-Chairman and Chairman of Sub-Committees of Classification; the former as a general rule to be an underwriter, the latter a shipowner.

The revisions thus briefly described were related in greater or less degree to the approach of an inevitable event—the merger of the British Corporation and Lloyd's Register of Shipping.

Something has already been said of the formation of the British Corporation in Glasgow in 1890, with a good deal of support from Liverpool and the ports of South Wales. It was a breakaway movement of a formidable kind, powerfully backed by shipowners and shipbuilders of eminence in the North. The members of its Technical Committee were in the top flight of their professions, and the Chief Surveyor over a long period of years, Dr. Foster King, was a leader in his own department. The Corporation's distinctive character arose largely out of its advanced attitude towards technical developments and its flexibility of outlook in the matter of the distribution of material in the ship's hull. It had made firm arrangements with classification authorities abroad and had many friends in all parts of the world. During the two Wars its services were freely used by the Admiralty and other Government Departments.

In the earlier days of the British Corporation, especially while led by that redoubtable shipowner of the old school, Sir Nathaniel Dunlop, its attitude towards the older Society had been at times more than defiant, but the general shipping community had clearly foreseen the inevitability of some sort of compromise. As early as 1911 the Society had made an approach to the Corporation, but there was apparently no great force of conviction on either side, and that moment of opportunity passed. When both bodies joined in setting up a Joint Aviation Advisory Committee, in the summer of 1932, it might have seemed that another opportunity had presented itself, but it was somehow not taken up. It was not until the Second World War neared its end that the first serious approaches to a merger were made.

The initiative was taken by Lloyd's Register. Its leaders had seen that there would be difficult days ahead for British shipping, and that the right policy was to concentrate forces throughout the industry and the societies that served it. Talks, informal and exploratory, took place between delegates from both sides, and these went so well that a joint statement was submitted simultaneously to the respective Committees concerned. Among other fairly obvious suggestions, this statement recommended the creation of a Joint Negotiating Body to go into all aspects of the proposed fusion. To this the main Committees of both bodies agreed.

The examination of the position was lengthy and detailed, but the Joint Body was able to issue a report in July, 1945. This recommended the merger and outlined a scheme for carrying it out forthwith. The General Committee of Lloyd's Register accepted at a meeting held on August 9th, 1945. Eight days earlier, however, a meeting of the British Corporation had failed to produce the necessary 75 per cent majority required under its constitution to give effect to the scheme. So the two Societies went on ploughing their separate furrows until an event that affected both in different ways forced the hands of the die-hards.

In the United States the American Bureau of Shipping had been growing in strength and forcefulness and had been extending its influence abroad. Indeed, the British Corporation had used the Bureau as its agent in many outports in which it could not itself afford to have separate representation. A series of negotiations failed, however, to reveal a *modus vivendi* among the three groups concerned—Lloyd's Register, the British Corporation and the American Bureau—and the British Corporation seemed to be left in the weakest situation.

Talks between the Society and the Corporation seemed desirable. More than that, the new Rules issued by the Corporation in 1947 and by the Society in 1948 had shown that their respective standards were converging. Conversations were resumed. The old report of 1945 was still useful as a basis of negotiation; and on March 28th, 1949, the shipping world was informed that the British Corporation would cease to exist as a separate entity and would be merged with Lloyd's Register under the title of Lloyd's Register of Shipping united with the British Corporation Register.

The fusion was contrived with a remarkable lack of fuss and friction. If there had to be a few honourable retirements, most of the British Corporation staff started to work happily with the Society's men and on the terms of service enjoyed by the latter. The dovetailing of appointments on the higher Committee level was contrived with good sense and without difficulty. The most extensive change took place in Scotland, where members of the Management Committee of the British Corporation, its headquarters in Glasgow, combined with the Glasgow Committee of Lloyd's Register to form a new Scottish Committee.

The Corporation's name is not now used in official nomenclature. Its Rules and practices, however, continued to be effective until May, 1954, when a set of unified Rules signalised the completion of a powerful union. The fusion meant that more than 90 per cent of the tonnage owned in Great Britain and Ireland in 1949 was classed with the now united Society, and that the combined staffs were surveying more than 94 per cent of the 2,115,000 tons gross under construction at the end of that year.

To the partnership the British Corporation made one contribution of special interest and value. It had developed a useful connection with the owners of those elongated freighters that ply on the Great Lakes of North America. When the Canadian Committees of the two societies were united, therefore, a Great Lakes Sub-Committee was formed. It still functions usefully—almost, one might say, on the fringes of rival territory—and its importance in relation to the new St. Lawrence Seaway is obvious.

CHAPTER 13   FOREIGN PARTS

IT has already been seen that Lloyd's Register of Shipping first sent
surveyors abroad in the early 1850's, in response to a request from
the maritime provinces of Eastern Canada, where the craft of wood
shipbuilding had started to flourish. It has also been shown that,
much about the same time, the Society was approached by shipping
people in the Low Countries to extend to them the benefits of its
services.

These were remarkable testimonies to the credit Lloyd's Register
had earned in less than 100 years: in only about 20 since the Society
had been reconstructed in 1834. They acknowledged Britain as a
fortress of excellence in shipbuilding, Lloyd's Register as the prime
expression of that excellence. The approaches from the Continent
were all the more flattering in that the Dutch in particular had a

maritime tradition fully as venerable as that of Britain and had been for a long time our very formidable rivals and even enemies. It is much to the credit of the leaders of commerce in Holland and Belgium— both countries with considerable colonial possessions in the East Indies and in Africa respectively—that they sought to follow the British lead, to bid for reasonable shares of overseas trade, and to emulate the high standards of construction and fitness embodied in the Rules of Lloyd's Register of Shipping.

The appointment of a Mr. Pretious from the London staff to be Surveyor for Holland and Belgium lasted from 1856 to 1859, and why he was recalled in the latter year and not replaced cannot now be known. Another seven years were to pass before Mr. L. Meyer succeeded him, with headquarters at Antwerp. The rapid development that followed has already been sketched, but the main features of the process must be recapitulated if the picture of the foreign establishment is to be seen as a whole.

During his first years of responsibility at Antwerp, Mr. Meyer had recommended the appointment of deputies or agents at the Dutch ports of Amsterdam, Rotterdam and Veendam, but this did not fully satisfy the leading merchants and shipowners in Holland, and in 1868 they sent to London, signed by 30 of them, a memorial suggesting the appointment of a resident surveyor at Rotterdam. The Society compromised by raising Meyer's deputies at the Dutch ports to the rank of Assistant-Surveyors. Within a year, however, they were given the status of independent officers. In Belgium and Holland, therefore, the first firm outposts of Lloyd's Register of Shipping in continental Europe were established.

The spread of the Society's influence throughout Europe was rapid thereafter. A special Sub-Committee formed in 1869 appointed surveyors at Trieste, Ancona and Venice, bringing Austria and Italy within the sphere of influence. Even if the Franco-Prussian War was a tragic distraction, 1871 saw the establishment of surveyors at Bordeaux, Hamburg and, in distant Australia, Melbourne and Sydney. A year later formal appointments were made to Copenhagen, Bergen and Genoa. Meanwhile, in 1869—the forerunner of a long procession to the Far East—a surveyor was sent from Quebec to Shanghai, the first on the continent of Asia. A condition of any surveyor's contract is that he must go wherever he may be sent.

From such beginnings the Society's influence overseas spread rapidly and so extensively that there were few substantial ports in the world at which it was not represented. As the standards of technical education and shipbuilding skill abroad improved, the Society was able to make increasing use of local technicians well-equipped to do its work according to the best standards of the main body of surveyors in Great Britain. They inherited a pride in high and detached standards; most of them were stubbornly loyal to Lloyd's Register when their native countries were invaded in the courses of two desperate conflicts.

No doubt the worthy merchants and shipowners of the Low Countries who sought the help of Lloyd's Register of Shipping during the mid-19th Century valued its services in the first place as an agency abroad. It was obviously useful to have representation of some sort in foreign parts where neither their own governments nor their own private enterprise had established anything quite like the Society's unique non-commercial service. Probably they were mostly concerned with the *ad hoc* survey and proper repair of ships damaged in distant parts. It should be noted that the first applicants for assistance were "merchants and shipowners"; there is no mention of shipbuilders taking part in the first approaches to the Society.

This was during the brief period in which shipbuilding practices abroad were hardly so advanced as those of Great Britain. British technicians had raced ahead of all others in the matters of iron, latterly steel, construction of hulls and the applications of steam as a propellant power. That advantage could not, however, last for ever.

Slowly but surely the continental shipbuilders, correctly following British practice, appeared as rivals to the British shipbuilders. They switched, more rapidly than in the conservative United Kingdom, from the native practices in wood and sail to metal and steam; and they were favoured by strong nationalist impulses. The day came towards the end of the 19th Century when the British near-monopoly of steam shipbuilding was being challenged from a dozen bases abroad. One Professor of Naval Architecture at Glasgow University, a cradle of the steamship, told the present writer that, at the turn of the century, the Japanese and Italian and German students in his classes far outnumbered native worshippers at the seat of learning.

The advance of the Society's influence overseas is perhaps best seen as a series of adjustments to a series of changes in the economic climate of what we nowadays call the Western World. If the merchants and shipowners of countries beginning to build for themselves required its various services, then Lloyd's Register of Shipping would always be available for consultation. It was desirable, however, to establish firmly a superior technical service of international standing, available for the survey and classing of ships wherever they might be. Whatever policies governments may seek to follow, the outlook of shippers throughout the world must be beyond the frontiers, and the shipowners and shipbuilders of most of the greater trading nations were well content to abide by the standards set up by the Society over a very long period of historical time. The ideal of collaboration on international lines was greatly encouraged by the growth in the number of the National Committees of Lloyd's Register from the period of the First World War onwards. It has been seen that an influential American Committee was formed in 1916, at a time when the British authorities were purchasing vast quantities of war materials in the United States. The outstanding success of this experiment encouraged the Society to extend the scheme, and in December, 1919, the Comité Français was set up in Paris. Swedish shipping and shipbuilding interests formed a National Committee in 1920, and that country, having no native registration society, has staunchly supported Lloyd's Register ever since. A year later National Committees were set up in Holland and Japan; the chain was further strengthened by the formation of a Danish Committee in 1930.

These National Committees were—to speak for the moment only of the pre-1939 position—much more than honorary bodies. They were made up of the leaders in underwriting, shipowning and shipbuilding in the countries concerned. The members were all men of wide experience and high responsibility who, whatever the classification system their country favoured officially, were determined to uphold the proved Rules of Lloyd's Register and enjoy for themselves the advantages of its unique international standing. As we have seen, the expansion of the Technical Committee in 1948 brought the National Committees into still more intimate touch with their colleagues in London.

And where stood Germany meanwhile? In general, the German Government carefully controlled its own shipping affairs. There was never any question of a National Committee being set up in that country; the Germanischer Lloyd was their chosen classification authority. Even so, the demand of German shipowners and shipbuilders for the Society's special services was so insistent that Lloyd's Register maintained a strong staff at Hamburg, with outposts at other shipbuilding ports and in the steel-making centres of the Reich.

The preliminaries to the First World War were conducted according to protocol, and no British members of Lloyd's Register staff abroad suffered much more than inconvenience. Even in the rough and tumble of the Second, only four surveyors, three British and one Dutch, fell into enemy hands. The brunt of discomfort fell on those officers and employees of the Society who were natives of countries occupied by the Axis forces or, as in the case of Italy and Japan, of nations that joined Germany against the Western Allies. What is quite extraordinary is the degree to which the Society commanded the loyalty of so many men who had lost their means of livelihood and were inevitably suspect by the occupying authority. It remains a fact, however, that in most occupied countries the native surveyors, exclusive or otherwise, were suffered to continue the work on which they had been engaged at the outbreak of war—a sincere if backhanded compliment to the standards of Lloyd's Register. (This applied particularly to ships being built for neutral countries.) There were to be no salaries from the source of power in London, but these officers drew on their savings and were admirably assisted by native firms—Cockerill's in Belgium for example—who nominally owed the Society fees for work done. The native Italian surveyors contrived to survive on what they called an *ad personam* basis—that is, nominally in private practice but as exponents of Lloyd's Register technique, much appreciated by native shipbuilders, war or no war.

On February 9th, 1941, the Society's office in Genoa was destroyed by naval bombardment, and the homes of several staff members were hit in this and subsequent attacks. The dealings of the Italian Ministry of Communications with the displaced officials were, however, reasonable, and while they were never comfortable and always hard-up, they scraped through somehow. Even when Italy collapsed, Genoa remained under German control, but Hitler had by this time too many anxieties elsewhere to worry much about an Italian port efficiently blockaded.

The war-time pressure bore much more heavily on the native officers in Belgium and Holland. It was natural that the Gestapo should see in any foreign outpost of Lloyd's Register a possible centre of espionage, and individual members of native staff had to survive many bad moments. Most succeeded by dint of lying low and getting on quietly with such work as the shipbuilders could give them.

The Rotterdam office was inevitably almost totally destroyed by the aerial bombardment of May 10th, 1940, after German seaplanes had come to rest on the river before its windows. As members of the staff made their way to see what of their records might be recovered they had the luck to encounter Mr. J. Rypperda Wierdsma, Chairman of the Holland Committee of Lloyd's Register. A meeting in his home was promptly arranged, and on the afternoon of May 17th several members of the Holland Committee and the surveyors, J. J. Schoo and L. Vuyk, worked out a taut plan whereby the Society's work might be carried on unostentatiously but usefully.

This worked sufficiently well until 1944, when funds ran out but, the discomforts of constant surveillance and meagre rations notwithstanding, the Dutch representatives of the Society fought a sturdy rearguard action and got through a surprising amount of useful work. One or two of them miraculously contrived to attend a course in electric welding at Nijmegen. If they were forced like their Italian colleagues to appear to be in private practice, or to be employed by the shipbuilders, the technical standards they upheld were those of Lloyd's Register.

The increase in the power of Swedish shipbuilding, and of the influence of Lloyd's Register in that country, make a rather curious tale. The first surveyor, non-exclusive, started work about the southern ports in 1874, but his base was Copenhagen, and the supervision of Swedish work was exercised from the Danish capital until 1877, when a non-exclusive surveyor was appointed at Gothenburg. The first exclusive surveyor there, V. C. Bülow, was appointed in 1900. The circumstances of the First World War favoured the Swedish shipbuilders, and they took to the construction of ocean-going vessels of size; the technical staff of Lloyd's Register in Gothenburg rose in number to five.

Sweden's strategic position in the Second World War was such that her shipbuilding and steel-making flourished, her advances in the uses of electric welding being notably swift. The overall advance in half a century is easily expressed in figures. For one exclusive surveyor in 1901 there were 36 in 1952. Swedish tonnage classed by Lloyd's Register amounted to 242,500 in 1901 and by 1959 had risen to 3,166,500 (87 per cent of the Swedish merchant fleet). The advance proceeds. A recent figure shows that the number of reports issued in a year, including various types of certificates, had risen from 150 in 1901 to 8,666 in 1958.

The history of the Danish connection with Lloyd's Register is of rather unusual interest, in that a non-exclusive surveyor was appointed to work from Copenhagen as early as 1871: that is, three years before he was called on to assume the oversight of the Society's work in the Swedish southern ports. The first Danish-built ship classed with the Society was the iron screw steamer *Rolf*, built by Burmeister of Copenhagen. That was in 1872, and to-day the great firm of Burmeister & Wain is in the advance guard of international shipping, especially in its applications of the diesel-type engine in very large ships.

The first exclusive surveyors were appointed to Copenhagen in 1901. Their number rapidly increased, keeping pace with the increase of Danish output. There were 17 on the roll in 1959. Tonnage classed with the Society in the first nine months of that year totalled 138,881, nearly 78 per cent of the country's whole output. Indeed, the National Committee for Denmark has remained in wonderfully good heart, the crises of the Second World War notwithstanding.

When the country was invaded in 1940 the Senior Ship Surveyor in Copenhagen, Mr. J. Hodgson, had to suffer the inevitable discomforts of internment, but with the firm support of the National Ministry of Trade and of a special Sub-Committee of the Danish Committee, with Mr. A. P. Möller as its Chairman from 1942 and Mr. H. P. Christensen of Elsinore always in the van, the native staff got through a large amount of work without serious interference. Apart from work on welded vessels, cold storage equipment and steel testing, the native surveyors supervised the construction of 22 new ships to the Society's class, with seven more still building when hostilities ended.

Seen in historical perspective, the situation throughout Scandinavia during the Second World War teemed with paradox, but two main factors were at work. In the first place, the occupying forces had no wish to halt native production of ships. In the second, the position of a neutral Sweden in the centre of the geographical system strangely complicated the problems of all the belligerents.

German rule in Norway was severe. The country's geographical position was of immense strategical importance, and the vast majority of the people, despite Quisling, were ready to go on fighting with every weapon they could seize. The position of the surveyors in Oslo was always uncomfortable. The office was threatened with closure; all classification work must go through Det Norske Veritas; and so on and so on, while the surveyors blandly pointed out that only the classification of Lloyd's Register was acceptable in Sweden. The bleak years passed, and food was scarce. Norwegian shipbuilders guaranteed a bank loan to cover bare running expenses, but the surveyors voluntarily imposed on themselves a salary cut of 20 per cent from April, 1942, onwards.

The lot of the single Norwegian surveyor at Bergen was an unhappy one. The German security officials were naturally interested in his doings, and he had on one occasion to endure a three-hour-long examination. Again his communications with Gothenburg were the subject of interest. He had sent information to London through Gothenburg; he must forward all his reports on ships through Germanischer Lloyd; in fact he must stop reporting to Gothenburg altogether.

Mr. Eide pondered this threat anxiously, and he made up his mind not to obey: a fine act of moral courage. He was fortified in his decision by the clearness of his conscience. He had not sought to communicate with London. His reports to Gothenburg concerned technical matters only, like those of the Oslo surveyors, and he reckoned that his own candour would save him in the long run, as indeed it did.

The chief factor in all these transactions in Denmark and Norway was precisely the neutrality of Sweden and the importance of Stockholm and Gothenburg as clearing centres for both sides. It was war in a vacuum perhaps, but it was still war, with many exciting and several dangerous moments. There were three British surveyors in Gothenburg, and on the senior of them, Mr. Townshend, fell heavy responsibilities.

The German invasion of Denmark and Holland virtually cut

Sweden off from the rest of the world. It was possible for a time to send letters round the world to London by way of Siberia and North America, but only routine matters could be dealt with in such a circuitous way. The isolation of Sweden became absolute when Finland and Britain were nominally at war and Japan launched the attack on Pearl Harbour. Naturally jealous of its neutrality, the Swedish Government applied its own postal censorship. To that the Germans added a blockade. Only by telegraph could there be any communication with the outer world.

Under the first shock of the invasion of Norway the British colony in Sweden hardly knew where it stood. Evacuation of the ports was considered seriously, but only for a matter of hours; a scheme to get the women and children out through Petsamo was abandoned. It was fairly soon apparent—an almost comic situation—that the neutrality of Sweden was valuable to both parties so bitterly at war elsewhere. Germany must have supplies of high-grade ore; Britain needed all it could get of Sweden's first-grade ball bearings. Both required for a variety of political reasons to hold a Swedish outpost.

In all these strange circumstances Mr. Townshend and his colleagues had to assume powers that would normally have been the sole concern of Head Office in London. In their efforts they were courageously backed by the Swedish Committee of Lloyd's Register under its Chairman, Consul-General Gunnar Carlsson. There will be something to say later on about the nature and bulk of their surveying work during the long years in exile, but the sensational aspects of their situation are irresistible.

As most students of Second World War tactics know, the German blockade of Sweden was never complete. British ships capable of very high speeds could and did get through to Sweden and come out again with invaluable cargoes of ball bearings and such. The postal blockade was at least partially broken by air services: in the first place by the Swedes themselves, using a Flying Fortress which, obliged to land on Swedish territory, had been roughly converted to ferry purposes; then by a courier service of R.A.F. machines. All communications had to be on flimsy paper, and it was impossible to transmit plans, but the isolation of the surveyors in Gothenburg was thus not complete.

Even movements of personnel, albeit furtive and highly dangerous, became possible. Consul-General Carlsson made several journeys to and from Great Britain during the war. On one of those an engine of the converted Flying Fortress caught fire while the machine was over Norway and made it an obvious target for the German A-A gunners. Their fire was accurate, but the aircraft got away over the North Sea, and then a second engine began to fail. The valuable cargo of ball bearings was jettisoned, but the worst was still to come. A third engine started to fail. Radio communication with the Air Ministry was established. It was decided that the Fortress could make only for a small, unlighted airfield in the Shetlands; air-sea rescue services were alerted. The run-in was made at length, after the crew had assembled in the nose of the machine and then rushed aft to keep the nose off the ground. Consul-General Carlsson ruefully admitted later that among the sweetest words he ever heard were just three in English out of the darkness in Shetland—"B——y fine landing". From that trip he returned more swiftly, but no more comfortably, in the bomb bay of a R.A.F. Mosquito.

Two more or less profitable attempts to run the German blockade were made by sea. The first, a brilliantly successful operation, took place during the winter of 1940–41.

A number of Norwegian ships had been caught in Swedish ports, and it was the idea of the British authorities that the fastest and most modern of these should be loaded with ball bearings and other high-quality products and sent out to try their luck. It was arranged that these ships should be fitted with devices that would allow them to be sunk quickly in case of attack, and large valves normally used in the pipe lines of tankers, that would allow a rapid inflow of sea water in the case of alarm were fitted in the ships' sides, in the holds and engine spaces. They did not have to be used. Five sizeable vessels thus equipped got through safely with their valuable cargoes.

A second effort in the following winter was less successful. In this case the Swedish shipbuilders, though well-disposed towards the Allies, felt it prudent to refuse a supply of valves, and other arrangements had to be made to ensure that the ships did not fall into German hands. This problem was solved by placing explosive charges in the sides of the ships, to be fired electrically if necessary from a single control in the captain's cabin. The fitting of these gadgets and the alteration of the ships were carried out in conditions of utter secrecy,

L

but largely in vain. The Germans got wind of the scheme and brought forward a legal action in respect of the ownership of the 10 vessels concerned. This delayed the sailing until the days were beginning to lengthen, and five of the blockade runners were promptly sunk in the Skagerrak. Another was sunk by air attack off the British coast. Two contrived to return to Gothenburg unharmed. Only two reached British ports in safety.

Before the war about 65 per cent of shipping built in Swedish yards was surveyed and classed by Lloyd's Register. The balance consisted almost entirely of ships built for Norwegian owners and classed by Norske Veritas. It was the strange fortune of war to confer on Lloyd's Register a near-monopoly of classification in Sweden, and it remains remarkable that Mr. Townshend and his assistants got through so much work in such strange circumstances. In the absence of full communication with London they had to be much of a law unto themselves, even to the point of issuing advice, if hardly instructions, to their colleagues in Denmark and Norway. They had to assume responsibility for the computation of freeboards and the issue of freeboard certificates. During the war period 3,250 hull plans and some 2,000 machinery plans were examined in the Gothenburg office.

Everything depended on supplies of materials. Swedish steelworks and manufacturers stepped up their outputs, but the Germans were progressively unable to keep their part of a trade agreement. The effects of Allied bombing of the German steelworks and transport system became obvious even in 1942; by 1943 the steel delivered from Germany and Belgium declined in quality. At length the German supplies began to dwindle and, even before the surrender, ceased altogether.

The story of Lloyd's Register in Sweden during the war is a strange one of survival, both for the Swedish shipbuilder and the Society, in artificial and difficult circumstances; and we may fairly see in it a demonstration of the strength of Lloyd's Register as a detached authority, absolutely neutral in all matters of technical concern. Even so, the lonely Surveyor in Bergen, reporting to London after the war, went out of his way to record the fact that Mr. Townshend in Stockholm had found time to send him an occasional and much-appreciated parcel of foodstuffs.

The recovery of the Society's positions abroad was a long and complicated business. The technical staffs faced an enormous backlog of tonnage built in occupied countries and then laid up for prolonged periods. Add the mass of shipping damaged but capable of repair, and the hands of the surveyors were full. The task of keeping the Register Book accurately posted became formidable. All such things were the tactical consequences of a long and destructive war; the higher direction of Lloyd's Register had to give serious thought to the re-establishment of its strategic position in foreign parts.

Several of the National Committees had, of course, survived intact or even in strengthened positions: in the United States for example. If the Swedish Committee had had to face appalling difficulties, its ultimate survival had in fact improved its standing in esteem. Three of the leading members of the National Committee were highly honoured by King George VI.

Other National Committees in the occupied countries automatically reconstituted themselves. There remained the delicate problems presented by the Society's relationships with the shipping communities in ex-enemy countries, Italy for instance; in countries long occupied and with governments inclined towards collaboration, France being the most important case in point; finally, in the utterly-defeated and occupied territory of Germany.

The first hint of the Society's awareness of the problems—and the possibilities—confronting it is to be found in a General Committee minute dated some months before V-E Day. This dealt with the position of the Bureau Veritas of France, after the long period of political confusion in that country. The trend of this report was no more than noted, the Chairman wisely observing that it would be well to keep the Paris office open at least until the French shipowners came to face the task of rebuilding their fleets. At the same meeting—in March, 1945—the Committee approved an arrangement whereby the Society's surveying duties in the Western Mediterranean region would be taken over by certain surveyors of the Ministry of War Transport, these officers to be ranked as Acting Surveyors to Lloyd's Register.

In considering the steps that followed the peace of 1945 it is important to remember that Lloyd's Register had acquired during its many years of existence a supra-national status.   For reasons already explained it operated influentially in countries that supported classification societies of their own—Italy and France, for example; in most other shipbuilding countries, though not in the United States nor in Japan, its influence was nearly paramount.   No man could foresee in 1945 how the Society's affairs were likely to rearrange themselves in a world sadly confused.

Oddly enough, the first approaches towards a renewal of better relations came from Finland and Italy, and we may be sure that the initiative in both cases sprang from the respective shipping communities rather than from the Governments concerned.   All such moves were treated with courteous caution in the first place, the Committee no doubt awaiting a clarification of the international situation, but when it was advised towards the end of 1946 that tonnage built in the considerable shipyards of Spain and Portugal was constructed according to the standards of Lloyd's Register to the tune of nearly 100 per cent, the first major post-war advance in the foreign field was promptly made.

This was the establishment of a strong Spanish Committee, inaugurated at a meeting in Madrid on October 28th, 1947.   (It might well have been called the Iberian Committee since Portugal was influentially represented on it.)   The function was attended by the Chairman, Sir Ronald Garrett, who took the opportunity on the same trip of visiting Bilbao and Lisbon as, later on, he and Lady Garrett went on to attend a series of more formal celebrations in Madrid.

The Spanish shipbuilding industry is not large by North European standards, but it is of venerable age, and it is increasingly productive. A steamship was built at Triana, Seville, as early as 1817, but it was not until the early years of this century that there was a real revival of naval and merchant construction.   For many years the Society was represented in Spain by non-exclusive surveyors at Barcelona, Bilbao, Cadiz, Cartagena and Seville.   The first exclusive surveyor, Mr. J. Pollock, was appointed to Bilbao in 1910.

The Civil War, followed by the Second World War, inevitably checked progress, but expansion since 1950 has been so remarkable that 20 surveyors of various grades now serve Lloyd's Register in the Iberian Peninsula.   Large passenger liners have been built at

Bilbao, while one yard at Ferrol and two at Cadiz have been putting out large tankers, two of 32,000 tons. Indeed, there was built at Valencia in 1958 a 13,000 ton cargo vessel for British owners. So Spain resumes her place in the world picture and, with her increasing drive towards hydro-electric production, the refinement of oil and the large output of steel in the Bilbao region, offers a widening field for the application of the Society's standards.

Soon after the Spanish tour Sir Ronald and his lady were off again to Australia and New Zealand.

The relationships between the Society and the countries of the Commonwealth would make a rewarding subject of separate study. The expansion of Lloyd's Register services in these distant realms is a tolerably exact record of their growth in independent trading power. The case of New Zealand is specially interesting, in that that country's development as a trading nation dates from the discovery of sound refrigerating processes whereby New Zealand's vast production of agricultural goods can be safely stored and carried over long ocean distances to distant markets. Urgent representations from the country's shipowners, underwriters and shippers undoubtedly influenced the Committee of Lloyd's Register to frame and issue in 1898 the first Rules governing the nature and installation of refrigerating machinery in ships.

For many years the Society's affairs in New Zealand were overseen by the combined Australian and New Zealand National Committee in Sydney, N.S.W. The formation of the separate N.Z. Committee recognised the unique importance of a country that on the average exports in a year 400,000 tons of meat, 165,000 tons of butter, 85,000 tons of cheese, and 1,500,000 boxes of apples; not to mention some 1,200,000 bales of wool. Apart from the British shipowning concerns that naturally made a bid for a share of this new trade, New Zealand developed its own far-sighted, always alert Union Steamship Company that has contracted out so much profitable work to British shipyards and controls a fleet of 65 vessels with a total tonnage of 226,318 gross.

The volume of work in New Zealand to-day requires the services of six exclusive surveyors stationed at the major ports and five non-exclusive surveyors at smaller places. Ship repairs and the examination of refrigerated cargo installations provide the bulk of the routine work, but there is much to do outside the marine department.

Latterly, the inspection services of the Society have been much in demand for the certification of components purchased abroad by Government and public authorities for new power stations, sewage works, bridges and cranes, along with the inspection of pressure vessels and the installations of the N.Z. National Airways. One way and another, New Zealand is a nearly perfect example of the manner in which the services of Lloyd's Register match the needs of an expanding trading community.

One does not think of South Africa as a shipbuilding country, and the new tonnage produced is small. On the other hand, Cape Town and Durban are terminal ports of great commercial—and strategic—importance, and there is always a heavy load of marine work to be done. The country's needs were served by non-exclusive surveyors until 1928, when Mr. A. H. Boyle was sent out from London to be exclusive surveyor, with an office in Durban. His headquarters were transferred in 1935 to Cape Town, but in 1949 the Society's principal office in South Africa was returned to Durban. The main reason for this was the development of great steelworks in the Transvaal, at Pretoria, Vereeniging, Benoni and, later on, Vanderbijlpark and Union Junction.

The manufacturers concerned sought one by one to be included in the Society's approved list. South Africa is now producing some two million tons of steel each year, and the Society saw fit in 1956 to set up an office at Vereeniging, specially to serve the steel industry. Here now are two surveyors, kept fully occupied on Land Division work and often obliged to use aircraft to cover the vast territories about their headquarters.

The Society's position in India and Pakistan is in many respects like that it occupies in South Africa. There is one shipyard capable of producing ocean-going vessels at Visakhapatnam, and one surveyor is permanently stationed there, but it is again a case of a vast sub-continent with terminal ports on the ocean routes—Bombay, Calcutta and Madras and, in Pakistan, Karachi and Chalna. The bulk of the marine work is thus concerned with periodical inspection and the supervision of repair work in such large establishments as the Garden Reach workshops in Calcutta and the Mazagon Dockyard at Bombay.

The first surveyor of Lloyd's Register in India was appointed to

Calcutta in 1874, and until the British withdrawal in 1947 only one or two additions were made to the staff. It is of interest that the number of surveyors in India increased after Mr. Nehru's assumption of office. Eleven exclusive surveyors now work in the country—six at Calcutta, three at Bombay, and one each at Madras and Visakhapatnam. The duties of survey in East Pakistan are carried out by the Calcutta surveyors.

The Commonwealth tours of Sir Ronald Garrett after the Second World War were of obviously constructive value. At the same time, the Society was extending its influence, usually at local request, to strange places all over the world. It is one thing to employ a non-exclusive surveyor at the head of some remote backwater; for him the representation of Lloyd's Register is usually only a part-time occupation, and such fees as he may pick up are useful but relatively trivial. It is quite another thing to appoint in a distant place a full-time exclusive surveyor, highly trained and salaried, with an office, a house and some sort of assistance thrown in. Even so, during the five years after V-J Day, the Society acceded to requests for the appointment of surveyors in many surprising corners of the world. And whether or not each of these establishments paid its way financially does not matter in the least. This wide extension of the outposts was the expression of the obligation on Lloyd's Register of Shipping to be supra-national in outlook and to be of assistance to international shipping in general.

The post-war uneasiness in Europe subsided slowly but surely. The French Committee came to active life again. The Registro Italiano was eager to sign an agreement that restored the old cordiality. The shipping community of Greece invited collaboration, and exclusive surveyors of the Society appeared again in Jugoslavian ports. The most remarkable feature of post-war developments, however—another of war's ironic paradoxes—was the resurgence of the two most heavily defeated powers, Germany and Japan, as producers on a large scale.

The Second World War was a sad interruption of a long relationship between Lloyd's Register and the Japanese shipping community. Japan was a latecomer in the shipbuilding field, but even in 1879—not so very long after the country had emerged from feudal isolation—Mr. Yonosuke Mitsui purchased the *Orduna*, built in Britain to the

Society's class two years before, and renamed her *Hideyoshi Maru*. During the mid-1880's the Kyodo Unyu Kaisha had 15 steamers built in Britain to the Society's class, and when these were being delivered, a surveyor was at once appointed to Yokohama to look after their maintenance surveys. A second office was opened at Kobe shortly thereafter.

The first ship built in Japan to Lloyd's Register class was the *Suma Maru* of 1,522 gross tons, put into the water by the Mitsubishi Co. of Nagasaki in 1895; and from then onwards, while Japanese ship-owners continued to have ships built in Britain, the native industry expanded. This growth was greatly favoured by the passing in 1906 of the enactment frankly called the Japanese Shipbuilding Encourage-ment Law. The output of the Japanese shipyards rapidly increased, but the standards of Lloyd's Register continued to prevail, the Society's staff, both British and Japanese, increasing accordingly. As noted, a Japan National Committee was formed in 1921. Then, in 1941, the curtain fell.

It was in 1948 that Lloyd's Register returned to Japan. Its experts helped to put the native shipbuilding industry back on its feet, introducing much that was new in design and technique; they made, in fact, a great contribution to the recovery that has restored Japan to a leading position in the tables of world production. For a time, the Society was authorised to assign freeboards and issue certificates to Japanese ships under the International Load Line Convention, but this power was removed when the native registration society, Nippon Kaiji Kyokai, was in 1951 given by the Japanese Government the sole power in this respect. Even so, in spite of so many fluctuations of influence, the name and authority of Lloyd's Register command respect in Japan, and Kobe remains one of the Society's busiest outports.

The economic and industrial affairs of Germany passed promptly after V-E Day into the hands of the Allied Control Commission, and it was not until January, 1948, that the General Committee of Lloyd's Register learned that German steelworks might shortly be permitted to start the export of steel for shipbuilding. A secure foothold in the new Germany was gained five months later, when the Control Commission agreed that Lloyd's Register should be an approved classification society on the Rhine: this on the unanimous recommendation of the delegates of Belgium, France, Holland and Switzerland.

So Germany's export trade expanded in increasing freedom, and while the national classification society, Germanischer Lloyd, was resuscitated, there was more and more work for the surveyors of Lloyd's Register. (It should be appreciated that much of the work of the surveyors in Germany has always been concerned with the testing of steel.) By 1952 the Society was assuring veteran native surveyors that, although nominally still employed on a purely temporary basis, they might be eligible for pension under the voluntary scheme; and it was decided at the same time that "suitable German nationals" might be appointed to the permanent staff.

In that year, indeed, the Society's position in Germany was shown to be both strong and stable. The shipbuilding returns indicated that of the 175 ships of 433,000 tons building in German yards in early 1952, well over 20 per cent were being constructed to Lloyd's Register class. The staff that numbered six in 1948 had increased to 30, seven of them British, 23 German; and two surveyors were stationed at Hamburg to deal with plans on the spot. This growth has been maintained: in 1959 the technical staff in Germany numbered 77.

In the summer of 1950 the Polish authorities required that the Society's surveyors be withdrawn from the country. The offices at Gdynia and Katowice were therefore closed, and the Society's funds in Poland were transferred to London. A year later the Government of Czechoslovakia ordered that the Society's office at Pilsen be closed, and that the surveyor there, Mr. Melichar, be regarded as *persona non grata*. The demand from Prague was that representatives of all foreign classification societies in Czechoslovakia should become part of an inspection service attached to the Czech Ministry of Foreign Trade.

This move provoked protests on the international level. Since the great firm of Sulzer depended largely on the products of the Czech steelworks and engineering shops, the Swiss Government sought to intervene, and there were strong representations from Dutch and Italian interests. Lloyd's Register of Shipping, however, firmly refused to meet the Communist demand and notified all parties likely to be concerned, the British Foreign Office included, that the Society would be unable to accept in a classed ship material from Czechoslovakia that had not been inspected by one of its approved surveyors;

and the General Committee made it clear that its decision was firm.

These ideological gestures proved more picturesque than effective in the long run. In 1957 the Polish Government suggested negotiations for the return of Lloyd's Register to their ports, and there to-day the Society's writ runs as strongly as ever it did. The Czech Government was slower in moving towards a compromise, and an envoy sent from Prague to London had the unenviable task of seeking to persuade the Society to resume its activities in a country from which, along with other foreign organisations, it had been unceremoniously expelled! Eventually, it was agreed that the work should be undertaken by surveyors from Austria—but it is still the standards of Lloyd's Register that are applied behind this end of the Iron Curtain.

These successes should not be considered as political triumphs. They represent a triumph of the Society in its wholly detached, supra-national capacity.

CHAPTER 14   CLASSIFICATION AND THE BOOK

A former Chairman of the Society, speaking before the Insurance Institute of London on the work of Lloyd's Register of Shipping, confessed that he did not favour the use of a word that has been used again and again throughout this narrative—the word "classification". The objection was not so eccentric as might appear in the given context. The term dates from the very earliest days of Lloyd's Register, when the qualities of ships' hulls and equipments varied widely and it was desirable to give the underwriter a tolerably exact notion of the risk he was being invited to take. Now, in mid-20th Century, and thanks largely to the Society's influence, there is infinitely less variation in the character of ships, and it is among the chief of the Society's aims to encourage the up-grading of all shipping towards the ideal ✠100A1 standard.

Classification remains the term in regular usage, and no influence is likely to depose it now. For the purposes of modern commerce, however, the description of any ship by the Society requires to be given in much more elaborate detail than was possible in 1760, even in 1834. Any entry in the Register Book as the public sees it to-day includes a set of abbreviated notations that, however cryptic in the layman's eye, tell the shipping man as much as he probably wants to know about the ship in question. If he requires a still more elaborate account of the details of any ship he will find it in the Appendix to the Register Book. If, like the busy underwriter, he requires almost up-to-the-minute information of a vessel's state, he can refer to the Supplement issued monthly or have his copy "posted" even more frequently.

The scope of these addenda to the Register Book proper will be indicated later on. The latter remains the central work of Lloyd's Register of Shipping; it could be called the shipping man's Bible. It is the perfect product of nearly two centuries of experience; its regular production is the masterpiece of a vast, complex and almost awesomely efficient organisation. It is the end-product of the work of the Society's ship and engineer surveyors, hundreds of them all over the world. How it all comes to pass must be understood in outline at least.

Any ship built to the Society's Rules and maintained in class is subject to periodic survey throughout her working lifetime, and every vicissitude of her career is filed in the Society's archives. The *dossier*, so to call it, begins to build up as soon as the shipbuilder's plans have been passed by experts in the Plans division of Lloyd's Register and seen to be in accordance with the Rules: these experts, if seeing good cause, marking in red ink on the various sheets their amendments and recommendations. That done, one set of the plans goes back to the builders, and one is handed to the surveyors who will supervise construction in the shipyard and engine works. The latter is the basic document in the eventual *dossier*. It is worth noting that at a busy outport such as Glasgow, the seat of the Scottish Committee, most conventional plans can be passed on the spot. So it is also in other large outports, such as Hamburg, Kobe, Gothenburg, New York and Copenhagen.

So the long process of building a ship is started; the surveyor with all his measuring instruments watching the daily increase from the keelson upwards, checking progress against the approved plans, crawling with his torch into hollow bottoms and dark tanks, shinning up and down ladders, and occasionally bumping his skull against very hard chunks of angled steel. In their own department, in the shops where the propelling machinery is being built, the engineer surveyors are going through much the same motions according to the rules of their craft; and it should not be forgotten that the steel to be used in the creation of the ship has been tested and passed by the specialist surveyors in the rolling-mills. In practice, a qualified ship surveyor in one of the larger shipyards of Clydeside or Tyneside may have four or five ships to supervise during construction and—the numbers varying—one or two, already launched, being engined and completed.

At length, however, the new ship is completed, runs her trials, is formally accepted by the owners from the builders, having been fully approved by the Committee of Lloyd's Register as a good ship worthy of the notation ✠100A1. Her name and particulars thus become entries in the Register Book. The surveyor's copy of the original plan, along with the other relevant reports and certificates, go into the archives in London: the story of her life begun in fair typescript. The basement of headquarters in Fenchurch Street is packed with thousands of files. In 1925 the Society acquired the site of the Church of St. Katherine Colman adjoining the Headquarters building and has now spread into Haddon House built thereon, but even that extra space is strained. The only concern at the moment, however, is that the life history of any ship classed with Lloyd's Register can be looked up and shown to an authorised person within the space of minutes.

For if the average ship of sound construction may have quite a long working life, she is subject to wear and tear and to accident. In terms of the Rules even the ship originally classed ✠100A1 must undergo special survey at the end of the first four years and at stated intervals thereafter; while the engineer surveyors are even more insistent on frequent inspection of main engines, boilers, propeller shafts and so on. *The Society, however, has no statutory power to enforce these Rules.* The system can work only on intelligent and friendly colla-boration between the responsible shipowner and Lloyd's Register of Shipping; and so it does work. It is obvious that a merchant vessel regularly engaged on long voyages to the Far East and back, or a liner keeping schedule on a busy passenger route, cannot be held for survey precisely on the date when an inspection becomes due.

In practice the Society accommodates itself to the shipowner's trading needs. Thus it is possible for any ship to undergo a portion of its periodical survey at, say, Glasgow, then the next portion at Liverpool, the next at Rotterdam, and so on. But the reports of the various surveyors involved follow her about, so to speak, and are filed with the *dossier* in the catacombs of Fenchurch Street, while the appropriate section of the staff of Lloyd's Register watches her progress through the stages of survey and issues the necessary reports from time to time.

It has been sufficiently shown that the main trend of the Society's Rules is always towards the maintenance of ships in class and their survival in the highest class, but the Register Book must also account for those cases of ships that must be criticised or wholly removed from class for one reason or another. A shipowner may, for quite valid reasons, wish his property withdrawn from class and, provided nothing serious in the way of survey or repairs is outstanding, the fact will be noted in the Supplement, and the accomplished fact will be recorded in the next Register Book.

Non-compliance with the Rules is naturally a more serious matter. In a case of failure to abide by the Rules the appropriate notation in the Supplement runs "CLASS EXPUNGED—Non-compliance with Regulations (date)", and in the next reprint of the Book proper the neglect is simply expressed as "LR class expgd. (date)".

Without turning these pages into a manual or handbook of procedure it would be difficult to convey to the lay reader any clear understanding of the science of classification in all its ramifications and subtleties, so numerous are the aspects of safety at sea the Society and its technicians must see to. Much has already been said about the leading part played by Lloyd's Register in the formulation of the International Load Line regulations. The Society is authorised to issue load line certificates, and some 8,000 ships hold such credentials: a high proportion of the world's tonnage. These certificates are valid for five years in the case of classed ships, four in the case of unclassed ships: the work so important that the organisation includes a separate Freeboard Department, which issues some 2,500 load line certificates annually for ships of some 50 countries.

This busy department is also responsible for the issue of certificates in respect of lifeboats and life saving equipment, fire prevention and fire fighting gear, stability, light and sound signals and so on. Since national standards of measurement differ—the American from the British, for example—tonnage capacities have to be worked out and certificates issued accordingly. It is enough meanwhile that Lloyd's Register of Shipping, acting for many foreign governments with or without native classification societies, does a large proportion of the world's work in these directions.

To appreciate the scope of all such activities one has to try to see the Society's headquarters as the clearing house of information pouring in from all quarters of the globe. The intelligence system, so to call it, is as perfect as could be. It is embodied in the Classification Department, which, with a staff of more than 50, corresponds with shipowners as occasion arises and processes the reports of surveyors for submission to the Committee. These reports come in at the rate of 700 a week on the average. The majority, of course, are concerned with routine matters, and once the technical experts included in the Classification group are satisfied with the surveyor's report, whether on the condition of a hull or of engine and boilers, authorisation by the Chairman of the Classification Committee for the issue of the appropriate certificate is more or less a formality. Of the average 700 cases weekly, however, perhaps 50 are of sufficiently serious concern to require the full attention of the Sub-Committee of Classification: such cases including the assignment or withdrawal of class or requests for postponement of surveys overdue.

This Sub-Committee of Classification is in effect the nerve-centre of Lloyd's Register of Shipping in its chief activity—the assurance of fitness in all ships classed with the Society. Its constitution and procedure perfectly exemplify the principle of detachment inherent in the very existence of the Register. It consists entirely of leading figures in the underwriting and shipowning worlds, so that any owner whose actions may not commend themselves is at least being judged by his peers: in fact, his own elected representatives. The Sub-Committee meets on Fridays in each week. Unpaid—let it be remembered— London members of the General Committee take turns on a rota system to attend five or six consecutive meetings at three separate periods throughout the year. Members of the Committees outside London attend at their convenience, but Sub-Committees also sit at regular intervals in Glasgow, Liverpool and New York.

This responsibility is carried to the point that combined meetings of the several rotas are held twice a year, so that uniformity of practice and procedure are assured. The system has another virtue. The Sub-Committee must rely on surveyors' reports, and any report lacking in precision may return to the surveyor with a polite but firm request for a less ambiguous statement of the case. The discipline has the excellent effect of encouraging firmness and precision in the work of the surveying staff.

In such ways, therefore, the Classification Department filters the mass of information pouring daily into head office. All decisions of the Committee are noted and "diary dated", if necessary, to be brought out for review as recommendations are fulfilled—or not fulfilled. The reports are then filed away with the ship's papers that have been building up year by year from the original plans. There is a hardboard box for each ship, a tall flat case to be stored and indexed with the thousands already in the basement. These records are not for any casual enquirer to see, but they may be produced for inspection by a prospective purchaser if the owner agrees; and the buyer could certainly not have a calmer or fuller report on the condition of the article for sale.

So any alteration in a ship's condition, or the mere fact of its maintenance in class, marches towards permanent record in the Register Book. From the Classification Department all details of new particulars go to the Publications Department, the necessary editorial agency within the system. It is this department which collates and distributes in printed form the information that can now be made available to all interested parties.

The Publications Department is that one through which the Society is most closely in contact with the lay world. Unless he be a specialist, the man in the street may never know of its existence, but its work is before him every day, even if only in the form of newspaper paragraphs. Indeed, this department must work with something like the speed of newspaper production in certain of its activities, and it must at the same time maintain the highest standards of accuracy in the assembly and presentation of facts and in the nice if underrated science of proof-reading.

The ultimate target of the department's effort is the annual production of the Register Book, a catalogue of world shipping as complete and accurate as human care can make it. On the way to that end, however, the experts in this branch have many other duties to attend to. They edit and correct the proofs of the Society's Rules and Regulations for Steel Ships, all the technical notices that go out from time to time, the Rules for Yachts and the periodical Instructions to Surveyors. They see to the translation and printing of the Society's Rules in French, Spanish and German. They collect from all over the world particulars of ships building, analyse these and publish them in statistical form every quarter. Another quarterly return is of casualties, including ships being broken up. This is summarised in an annual publication, while another annual is a return of launchings during the year.

The statistical work of the Publications Department is only second in importance to the production of the Register Book, and the mass of tables it produces has made it probably the most important information centre of its kind in the world, able at any moment to satisfy the enquiries, whether commercial or purely historical, it receives in large numbers from the Press, from industrial concerns, from authors, students and the remote but numerous enthusiasts who dote on maritime lore. Government and international bodies look to the statistical returns of Lloyd's Register for information about trends in the world shipping situation; professional statisticians all over the world rejoice in them.

Much of the information embodied in these returns is gathered, of course, from the Society's own surveyors, but Publications seek their riches through direct correspondence and by the circulation of printed questionnaires. All official lists of ships, British or foreign, are closely scrutinised. Foreign registers and all shipping periodicals are watched by trained observers. It would be hard for any seagoing ship in the world to slip through this mesh unnoticed.

The annual issue of the Society's Tables of World Fleets is a peak moment in the publishing year, but it is still a by-product of the labour that goes into the main effort: the regular publication of the Register Book. The Tables, indeed, are just a sort of distillation, through a mechanical card-sorting system, of the huge mass of information collected for that chief purpose.

Something has already been said about the character of the Register Book in the early days, and illustrations of specimen pages

M

should have helped towards an understanding of its development. Inevitably, the growth of world shipping, the increasing complexity of the modern ship, and the demand for more and more detailed information have brought about many typographical changes, and changes in the size of the page and the weight of paper used, since the Book of 1764–65–66, "printed by W. Richardson and S. Clark in Fleet Street," first appeared. The Book is still "posted" by hand, changes entered almost daily. In effect, the importance of "posting" has tended to decrease with the now regular issue of the printed monthly Supplement to the Register that has a cumulative value over any working year and is the document of greatest use to those, such as underwriters, who must follow the market closely.

At one period the Society embarked on an ambitious project to put out a volume separate from the Register Book and much wider in scope. This, by a decision of the General Committee in 1885, was to be the "Universal Register", with particulars of all seagoing ships in the world above 100 tons, irrespective of classification. The first volume appeared in May, 1886, a work of monumental proportions, to which a key was printed in English, French, Dutch, German, Italian, Norwegian and Spanish. Its life was short; only four annual editions were put out; and in 1890 the Committee decided on a complete remodelling of the Register Book proper, to make it in fact more comprehensive than the "Universal" edition.

This now appears in four volumes, of which three are mainly of specialist interest. Volumes III and IV are really directories, the first of shipowning concerns throughout the world, the second of shipbuilding and repairing establishments, dry docks and so on. Volume II is the Appendix to the Register Book proper, supplying for those who require it more elaborate technical information than is included in the majestic masterpiece, Volume I.

This, with an unbroken history of 200 years behind it, has evolved as one of the world's supreme works of reference, universally used and trusted. It contains a list as complete as can be ascertained of all seagoing merchant ships in the world of 100 tons and larger whether classed by Lloyd's Register or not. The number of ships thus listed is more than 36,000.

The noble Register Book has an attractive little brother—twin brothers, in fact. Something has already been said about the emergence of a Yacht Section within the Society and of the first appearance in 1878 of a Register of Yachts. The sport became popular in the States, and enthusiasts on that side of the Atlantic persuaded the Society to inaugurate, in 1903, a separate Register of American and Canadian Yachts. Both suffered in continuity of publication during the two World Wars, but both were duly reborn and survive in an excellent state of health.

The character of the yachting world has changed vastly since 1878. The original rules of the British Yacht Racing Association, once as the laws of the Medes and the Persians, have been much modified by international agreement, after various sets of negotiations in which Lloyd's Register took a prominent part. The major changes, however, have sprung out of fluctuating economic conditions. There are not many men nowadays, on this side of the Atlantic at least, who can afford to build anything comparable in grandeur and elegance to the great steam yachts of Queen Victoria's latter and Edward VII's earlier years; nor shall we ever see again the great, and very expensive, racing machines of the J-Class that delighted the eyes of longshoremen up till 1930 or thereabouts. On the other hand, the same economic pressures, coupled with increasing densities of population and congestion on the highways, have sent more and more simple people to discover pleasure in sailing and racing small craft and brought about a large increase in the number of yachting and sailing clubs.

This general tendency was recognised by the Society shortly after the Second World War, and in due course yachting interests were taken out of the Classification Department and a new Yacht Section was set up. An active Yacht Sub-Committee of Chairman and eight other members was appointed and an administrative staff assembled under a Yachting Manager. Expert yacht surveyors attend to the technical side of the business. Any yacht of size can be built under the Society's survey and be awarded the coveted ✠ notation, like any passenger liner or giant tanker. The practice in this department is so resilient, however, that its available services are nicely geared to meet all the reasonable needs of the yachtsman of moderate means: that is including the engines, main or auxiliary, of his little ship.

In the nature of things, there is much buying and selling of the smaller sort of yacht, and the prudent buyer at least may require a Condition Survey before taking over a new boat. Lloyd's Register therefore offers him expert service in examinations in greater or less degree of severity. It is even "prepared to carry out a superficial examination of the hull in order to be in a position to advise on the type of survey considered necessary in the particular case, or"—an ominous phrase!—"whether it is worth while going on with a survey at all." At the same time, the rule of absolute detachment always prevailing, the regulations lay it down firmly that the Society cannot take part in arbitrations, and that its servants are forbidden to volunteer estimates of prices.

Much, but not all, of this yacht work is in the good old tradition of building in wood, and the yacht surveyors are happy specialists in a pleasant branch of construction. Now hulls are being built of light alloys, plastics, resins and so on, and something like mass production of dinghies and small speedboats has arrived; and so a range of new surveying and classification problems has to be studied.

In the nature of things, the compilers of the Register of Yachts can look to surveyors' reports for particulars of only a small proportion of entries. The 1959 edition of the British book and its supplements listed some 9,000 yachts of all types—sailing, auxiliary and motor— and the organised classification of so many small craft is obviously out of the question. After all, the number of yacht and sailing clubs was nearly trebled during the 20 years from 1939. Later editions of the Yacht Register have included lists of fixtures in every significant centre of yacht racing throughout the United Kingdom, from the sublimity of Cowes to an assembly of dinghies in an East Anglian estuary.

The Register of American Yachts, published through the Society's office in New York, deals with craft owned in the United States in the same manner as the British book. It also lists particulars of Canadian yachts. More than 8,500 Canadian and American craft are thus listed in the American Register; so that, taking the European total into account, the Society can account in one way or another for fully 17,500 yachts—surely a majority of the world total in that class.

So many publications represent a formidable job of printing, the substance of a contract that even the largest firms in that line might covet. It was seen at an early stage, however, that the needs of the Society could best be served by the establishment of printing works of its own, especially since the job of producing the Register Book alone required special typographical equipment and since the printer should ideally be in immediate and direct touch with the departments at Head Office that supply him with his material. Bernard Waymouth argued forcefully in these senses, and in October, 1889, a site in Southwark Street was purchased. There a Printing House was built and equipped in time to produce the Register Book and the Yacht Register for 1891.

In the nature of things, the original plant was brought up to date from time to time as printing machinery was improved and the scope of the Society's publications increased, but the old place served its purposes very well until the Luftwaffe started to attack Central London in the early years of the Second World War. In April, 1941, bombs fell on the building. Two top floors were wrecked, the Composing Room and the Posting Department gutted, while some 20 per cent of the standing type required for the production of the Register was destroyed. This calamity occurred while the Register Book was being reprinted for the year, but by one of those miracles of improvisation characteristic of the period its appearance was delayed by only two months.

The wounds were not mortal, so gallantly did the managers of the Printing House and their veteran and highly skilled workers fight through a long period of emergency, but it became obvious when the war was over at length and the tasks of reconstruction must be faced that the old Printing House could not be conveniently re-established in Southwark. The General Committee therefore turned, as so many minds were then turning, to the notion of building outside the city. In the issue, after much investigation and hard thinking, it was decided to set up the new Printing House in the industrial area of Crawley New Town in Sussex, where there were at once ample room for a modern factory in agreeable surroundings and first-rate housing accommodation for the staff. The lease of a two-acre site fronting Manor Royal, the main thoroughfare of the industrial estate, was signed in 1951.

The Crawley Development Corporation had already evolved a standard factory unit. This was found to be suitable in general for adaptation in a modern Printing House, with a separate block for the Society's growing Research branch, and the work was confidently entrusted to the Corporation's architects, with Mr. J. S. Hartley, A.R.I.B.A., chiefly concerned. In May, 1953, Lady Garrett laid a

Commemoration Stone near what is now the main entrance to the building; the place was given the name of Garrett House in compliment to the then Chairman, Sir Ronald Garrett. By the end of that year all the printing departments were installed and in operation, and the work was completed in the summer of 1954.

The Printing House is a seemly creation in the best modern manner. Quite apart from the airiness and light of the working spaces, good taste and a sense of history informed the decoration of the approaches to the administrative offices. The east interior wall of the stair landing carries a striking bas-relief—of a printer at work at an antique press—by James Woodford, R.A., the artist responsible for the Queen's Beasts in Westminster Abbey at the Coronation. Above the sweeping stairway that leads to the first floor, the west wall carries, in white and blue, the lines of the Clipper ship *Thermopylæ*, designed by Bernard Waymouth. The essential function of Lloyd's Register of Shipping is further symbolised on the terrazzo floor below by an elegant compass design set in mosaic.

This is altogether a place to rejoice the hearts of all who have known the smell of printer's ink and love that craft. The layman must not, however, be burdened with a technical account of the equipment of this typographical temple—the battery of Monotype machines, that of the more conventional Intertypes, the great range of flat-bed printing machines for all manner of specialised jobs, and the rest of it. The establishment fully employs more than 100 men and women on the administrative and mechanical sides. Although Crawley is 30 miles to the south of London, contact is maintained between the Printing House and Fenchurch Street by a regular service of both messengers and van.

It is here that one may see the "posters" at work—that special body of skilled workers, so often referred to throughout this history. Their function is to insert into copies of the Register Book, and at high speed, day-to-day corrections of the particulars it contains. In the very earliest days, when the circulation of the Book was small, these corrections were made with pen and ink, and no doubt the revised copies could quickly be circulated among subscribers within the City of London. To-day, the number of subscribers requiring "posted" copies is limited to a group of underwriters, insurance companies and shipowners, but these require for their professional purposes the latest information as to changes in the composition of the world's merchant fleets and even in the characters of individual vessels—even if many of the entries nowadays are confined to the melancholy phrase, "Broken Up". It is surprising how many changes of fortune are continually taking place: about 900 in each week on the average.

"Posting" is therefore an incessant task. The worker in this field is provided with a set of cases, each bearing a correction in type, and it is his task to go through Book after Book, imprinting the correction against the older particulars of the ship affected. The need for absolute accuracy in the job is obvious, but to see it being done by deft hands under the guidance of quick eyes is rather to be impressed by the realisation, surely dramatic, that into this single room of a printing establishment in Sussex there pours daily a stream of information regarding even slight changes in the world shipping situation, be it the result of a collision off the distant shores of Tierra del Fuego or the consequences of a cyclone revolving near the Philippines.

Indeed, the magnitude and scope of the Society's work is more easily appreciated in Garrett House than at any other point within the organisation. Within the labyrinth of Head Office, or even in the larger outport offices in Britain and abroad, the stranger may well be aware of a great deal going on but still be puzzled to determine to what end the various avenues are leading. It is in the Printing House that, as channelled through the Publications Department, the masterpiece is made visible in its bulk and variety—a massive witness to the superb, exhaustive services Lloyd's Register of Shipping renders to the mercantile communities of the world.

CHAPTER 15   THE LIVING ORGANISM

THE Head Office that Lloyd's Register of Shipping built for itself
in the last years of Queen Victoria's long reign is a handsome
building of its period, but it is now something of a survival in a City
area in which, after the ravages of war, the office blocks of the
Brave New World rise high, white and rectangular, equipped with
fast and silent lifts that seem to expel the caller towards his objective
on gusts of compressed air. The interior arrangement of No. 71,
Fenchurch Street, is far from "functional". It rambles, and the most
alert visitor does well to entrust to a uniformed Messenger the task of
navigation along the corridors and up and down the staircases.

As the work of the Society increases in scope, so do the departments
proliferate. The realists say that Lloyd's Register will simply have
to rebuild some day, but there are many others who would mourn

the passing of a place in which the exercise of a function wholly expressive of the British genius in shipping is matched by the furniture of a period that used solid wood and polished metals, heavy doors and stout furniture, stained glass and painted ceilings to express a proper sense of dignified responsibility. The decorative dignities of the Board Room apart, there is the perfect atmosphere of a very old and exclusive club in the L-shaped Smoke Room, in which the great ones of the General Committee hobnob between meetings; and there is an even more compulsive feeling of a living organism in the long dining room on the first floor where the Society's higher officers in both the technical and administrative branches meet for luncheon at a long table—to discuss technical problems if they wish, or just to estimate Surrey's prospects of winning the County Championship once again. Everywhere are pictures, either of great men of the shipping world or of maritime occasions. Some are good and valuable; all are interesting.

Working conditions apart, it would be strange indeed if a characteristic atmosphere had not developed within the Society's Head Office in the course of 200 years: a sense of belonging to a great institution, a solidarity rooted in pride and loyalty. These are imponderable qualities, to be sure, and however it may be in the outports, the technical and administrative staff of some 400 men and women at Head Office must live at great and widely-spaced distances all over the vast spread of Greater London, each with his or her separate environment and set of interests. In the nature of their calling the members of the surveying staff are mostly birds of passage and cannot contribute steadily to the corporate life.

Happily, there exist among the Society's records certain books and pamphlets to declare the existence within the staff of venerable loyalties and traditional customs, with each generation throwing up its own crop of dominant or picturesque personalities, and that long before the move from White Lion Court to Fenchurch Street. One of the decided "characters" of recent years, the late R. J. Sladden—in his official capacity Clerk to the Sub-Committees of Classification, out of office hours a pillar of sporting and social groups within Head Office staff—found time some years ago to conduct research in the older Minute Books of the General Committee and to discover what he described as "a wealth of domestic detail". His notes made up the substance of a paper he read before the Staff Association during the 1948–49 session. It was very formally entitled "Notes and Anecdotes on the Society's Staff during the Victorian Era", but there is much happy reading in it.

Sladden with his strong sense of history perceived that the reconstituted Society of 1834 was a delicate plant, insecurely rooted in the soil that had been soured during the bitter wars between the Red and Green Books. He is much concerned with the financial aspects of the merger, but his eye for the humanities is acute. How else could we have learned that the fusion of the Registers and consequent dismissal of staff caused hardship of a most pathetic kind? Witness the case of John Inville who petitioned the Provisional Committee in February, 1834, for financial help. He had been appointed a junior clerk to the Underwriters' Register in 1765, almost at the very beginning of scientific classification, and had been appointed a Secretary in 1799. Now, at the age of 82, he suffered from cataract in both eyes and was wholly without means, and the Provisional Committee was quite without funds to give him some sort of help!

It has been said more than once that Sir Andrew Scott, 65 years in the Society's service, held the record for continuous fidelity to it. That is not so. This pathetic John Inville served for 68 years on end, and Henry Adams, latterly Chief Clerk until he died in 1887, for 72 years. It is more interesting that Adams had worked beside Inville and Scott beside Adams—a chain of association spanning 175 years.

It was a peculiarity of the premises in White Lion Court that the boundary between the parishes of St. Peter-upon-Cornhill and St. Martin Outwith ran through the building, one of the boundary plates situated within the Board Room itself. Periodically the place was invaded by a cheerful party of Church dignitaries and perhaps two-score Charity Lads bent on "beating the bounds" with the long canes they carried for that purpose. This was an affront to the vast dignity of Henry Adams, and the regular encounter between his pomposity and the pertness of the boys was greatly appreciated by his colleagues, even by grave and revered members of Committee. By an eventual compromise the beaters came to accept the Head Messenger's assurance that the boundary plate was securely *in situ* in the Board Room, but it was long before the boys stopped banging on the outer door and shouting, deliberately to disturb the renowned stateliness of the great Chief Clerk.

The atmosphere of those days is now recognisably Dickensian. The old Minute Books seem to throw up precisely the sorts of "characters" and incidents in which the novelist delighted. After all, there seems to be fair warrant for the legend that Dickens, visiting his friend Thomas Chapman, the Chairman for so many years, was taken with the name Snodgrass under a portrait and adopted it for his own literary purposes. One may fancy that he found in the office in White Lion Court, in its earliest days at least, the sort of London setting in which he excelled. That office was in the first place a make-shift affair—two rooms on the first floor, two on the second, a room in the attics and a coal cellar. Here worked four surveyors (one Ship-wright and three Nautical), the Secretary and three clerks, a small squad to post the Book and do jobbing printing on the side, and one messenger. These premises were lit by candles until 1847.

The lot of a messenger in mid-19th Century was happily described by Jabez Barrett, latterly Head Messenger, who retired in 1911:—

> "The waistcoat was a bright red, which at first I thought to be very grand and conducive to importance, but, being called upon to take the waterside and East End walks, collecting and delivering the Register Books, my dignity was grievously offended, for being only a youth and necessarily having to pass through some very select avenues and choice alleys in the neighbourhood of the docks, my red waistcoat was a great attraction to the young ladies of these districts, and was the cause of remarks, pungent and sometimes very embarrassing. On one occasion I was quite surrounded and received many affectionate epithets, so on my return to the Office I told the Chairman and asked him if he had any objection to its colour being altered, and he most considerately consented to the alteration as at present, the red waistcoat finally disappearing."

Another amusing outcome of Mr. Sladden's researches was his discovery of the identities, and characters, of the two watermen engaged for services in the Port of London by the reconstituted Society. Paid £75 a year each and "annually furnished" with a jacket and badge; each allowed the help of a boy at £10 a year "with a Jacket and Trousers," they were Nathaniel Archer, who had worked for the Red Book previously, and James Buxton, formerly employed by the Green Book.

This division of the spoils of office, though tactful, did not work out very well. In 1839 Nathaniel Archer was dismissed for faking a medical certificate, leaving his boat in charge of the apprentice, and working the while behind the counter of his own alehouse. When the boat service was discontinued in 1841 James Buxton was given a job as messenger at White Lion Court. He was one of those referred to in the testimony of Jabez Barrett, thus:—

> "I was very unfortunate in the two superior officers in my department; one was a very old man who had been a Thames Waterman, utterly lacking in the milk of human kindness, having on one occasion, with over £20 sewn in his pocket, turned his starving married daughter away from the door, and the other man of no calibre whom the chosen few used to soak with alcohol and then sit him on the table in the Surveyors' room to make speeches."

Such blithe scenes could hardly be witnessed in No. 71, Fenchurch Street to-day, but the anecdote suggests the parlous state of the Society's affairs immediately after the fusion. It was at this critical juncture, towards the end of 1836 to be precise, that one of the Society's junior clerks fled to France after embezzling more than £700. The loss of this sum, apparently trivial to-day, was a heavy blow to the struggling body; this was also the occasion of Thomas Chapman's renowned gesture of consideration towards the staff by advancing cash from his own pocket to pay salaries before Christmas that year. Does Mr. Sladden spoil the story by revealing the fact that the Society still had in hand a tidy reserve of £1,000 in Exchequer Bonds?

The first London Shipwright Surveyor appointed after the amalgamation was George Bayley, a shipbuilder from East Anglia. He was not given the title, but he was in effect the Principal of the 63 surveyors, 13 of these exclusive, appointed after 1834. If the Chairman had had to dip into his own pocket to pay the salaries at Head Office during an emergency, it seems astonishing that Bayley received salary at the rate of £500 a year, calculated by Sladden to be worth, with his allowance for damage fees, £700 a year—a goodly emolument in that period. This officer was, however, a man of the highest competence if quick in the temper, and his integrity was thoroughly tested when, in 1839, he reported to the Committee that an envelope containing two £5 notes *and addressed to his wife*, had been left at his house in Addington Road, Camberwell.

Badges issued in 1834 and 1841 to Watermen employed by
the Society to row Surveyors to ships in the London Docks

It was never revealed, apparently, what favour was expected by the anonymous correspondent, but the Society promptly inserted in the *Shipping and Mercantile Gazette* an advertisement to the effect that "unless the party who has made the great mistake" came forward to explain his motive, the money would go to charity. Here was the making of a newspaper scandal, and there duly appeared in the *Gazette* a highly tendentious but anonymous letter, in which the writer sought, by describing the design of the seal on the offending letter and piously protesting against the dastardly attempt to involve "an amiable and respectable lady," to identify the culprit. But there were no bright lads in the Fleet Street of those days to follow up such a promising story. The Society let the matter drop and sent one of the £5 notes to the Merchant Seamen's Orphan Asylum and the other to the Seamen's Floating Hospital.

The advertisement in the *Shipping and Mercantile Gazette* was signed on behalf of the Society by Charles Graham, Secretary. It is now seen that this appointment, made in 1837, started an overdue reorganisation of methods in White Lion Court. Graham had worked in the Admiralty and brought to his new post a proper Civil Service regard for procedural order. Sladden notes, for example, that only with Graham's arrival were the Minutes of the Committee properly indexed. He set up a system of regular communication between surveyors and Head Office and arranged for the organised issue to subscribers of alterations to the Rules; and it has been found that several formal documents used within the Society to this day are worded very much as Graham drafted the originals more than 100 years ago. He was an invaluable henchman to Thomas Chapman, and these two pushed the Society's affairs along briskly. It is pleasant, if irrelevant, to know that Graham was obliged in 1844 to deal with a letter from Jersey, with 13 signatories, to the effect that the Society should introduce into the Register Book some mark to distinguish ships wholly manned by teetotallers!

The periodical outings of the Visitation Committee were important features of life within Lloyd's Register of Shipping during those early days. These perambulations round the outports were invariably led by Thomas Chapman in person, one of the London surveyors in attendance, and they were more than amusing outings. They proved to the surveyors working in remote places that they belonged to a

173

Society of increasing stature in the national scale, and it is on clear record that each tour, as the financial position improved, was made the occasion of a review of salaries. Once more: the importance of Chapman's devotion to the Society's affairs during the period of development in mid-19th Century cannot be over-estimated. Those long trips were at the expense of his private concerns. They could be tedious; and the round of the Scottish ports could be nearly an ordeal, the trains from Scotland back to London occasionally running as much as a day late.

Charles Graham died in May, 1855, and the General Committee sent his widow a copy of the Resolution in which they had expressed their sense of loss. The lady's reply is a model of dignity in the epistolary style of the period, and her reference to her reduced financial state is delightfully subtle. (We do not need to conclude that her hint persuaded the Committee into granting Mrs. Graham an annuity of £200. They could manage these things gracefully in that period of manners.) Graham's death came at an awkward time, just when the first Iron Rules had to be formulated and the Society's recommendations regarding the qualities and uses of the metal were being disputed by members of the manufacturing trades. This, however, was one of the inevitable ebbs in the tide of affairs, and during the early 1860's the Society took on a group of young men destined to become its pillars and to play fine parts in its expansion and growth in esteem.

Bernard Waymouth had come into the Society's employment in 1854. Failing in his application for the surveyorship of Cumberland, he had been consoled with a post as assistant surveyor in London. Principal Surveyor in 1871, he was to draw up the Society's Rules for Composite Ships. Then, by an oddity of promotion not uncommon within Lloyd's Register in those days, he was appointed Secretary in succession to George B. Seyfang in 1872; and in that capacity he had much to do with the establishment of the first Pension Scheme in 1884. Meanwhile, the staff position had been strengthened by the arrival on the scene of Benjamin Martell and Harry J. Cornish. These two formed with Waymouth a formidable triumvirate that greatly enhanced the standing of Lloyd's Register.

Cornish and Martell first attracted attention to themselves in an odd way. In 1863 the Committee offered prizes for the best set of

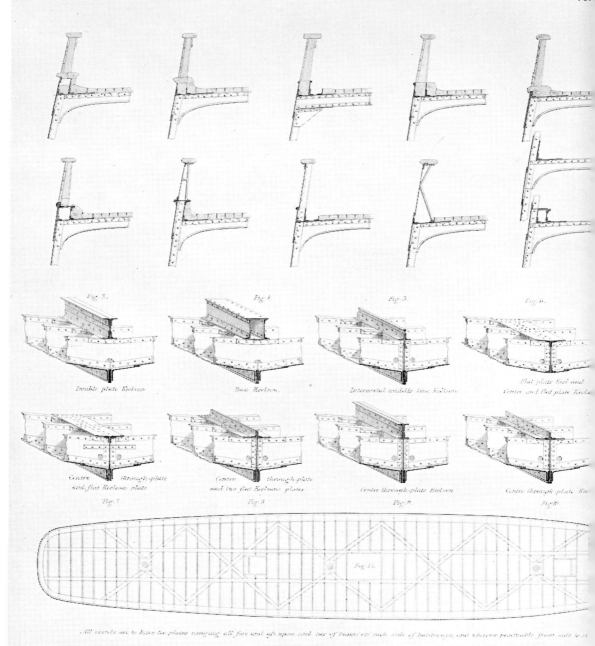

Drawings by Mr. Harry J. Cornish to illustrate the Rules for Iron Ships, 1863

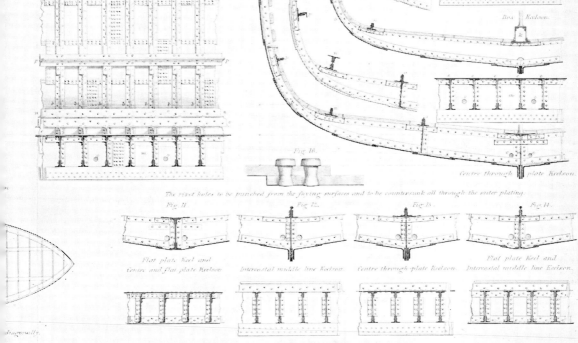

Fig. 2.

Fig. 1.

1000 Tons with three tiers of Beams

800 Tons with two Decks

Half Midship Section of a Vessel under 200 Tons with a single Deck.

Single plate Keelson.

Box Keelson.

Centre through plate Keelson.

Fig. 16.

The rivet holes to be punched from the faying surfaces and to be countersunk all through the outer plating.

Fig. 11.   *Fig. 12.*   *Fig. 13.*   *Fig. 14.*

Flat plate Keel and Centre and flat plate Keelson.   *Intercostal middle line Keelson.*   *Centre through plate Keelson.*   *Flat plate Keel and Intercostal middle line Keelson.*

drawings in illustration of the revised Iron Rules. This was won by Harry J. Cornish, whose delicate drawing of the "Lady" so long graced the Society's letterhead and publications, and who was always in demand for complimentary documents, menu cards and the like. The Committee was so pleased with the results of the competition, it decided that all 12 entrants should be given a prize; and one of these went to young Benjamin Martell. As we have seen, Martell was in 1872 appointed Chief Surveyor, as the title ran then, and did work of outstanding brilliance in the matter of load line regulations. Cornish had to linger long as his principal assistant until 1900, when he was appointed Chief Ship Surveyor, retiring from that high post in 1909 after 47 years of devotion to the Society's interests. He is still remembered as a man of unusually charming personality.

There had come upon the scene in the meantime one of the most remarkable personalities in the human history of Lloyd's Register of Shipping. This was Andrew Scott, latterly Sir Andrew—the perfect specimen of the able, persistent, dominating "lad of parts", such a figure within the administration of the Society and as a personality that those who worked under him still seem unable to decide whether his memory should be cherished with admiration or awe.

He had come under the attention of the General Committee while still a small boy in the Glasgow office: a Minute of 1873 recording that, in response to a communication from the Glasgow surveyors, "Andrew Scott be allowed a salary of £50 per annum, provided his handwriting be satisfactory". There was never anything far wrong with Andrew Scott's handwriting and nothing at all with either his clevernesss or devotion to duty. We merely note that nearly a pound a week was a very good wage for a boy in 1873 and an outstanding mark of appreciation of his qualities.

It would appear now that the wise eye of Thomas Chapman was upon this prodigy, for in 1874 the Chairman brought him to London to help in the editing of the Register Book during the illness of the Chief Clerk, Henry Adams. Scott was then 17 years of age; having the national gift of making himself indispensable, he never looked back—in both senses of that worn phrase. Bernard Waymouth was shrewd enough to take the lad over as his confidential clerk and after Waymouth died young Scott became Chief Clerk, in 1892. It was inevitable that he should succeed Arthur G. Dryhurst as Secretary after the latter's death in 1904. Andrew Scott was a masterful person, and it is all the more interesting that the dwindling company of men who worked under him and remember him well invariably mention, with appropriate chuckles, his enthusiastic patronage of Lloyd's Register Cricket Club.

This association of ideas is not quite so absurd as may appear at a first reading. All great institutions in good heart develop their own inner life; and as Lloyd's Register grew in strength and influence and the staff greatly increased in numbers during the second half of the 19th Century, so the corporate sense grew among the younger people working under the same roof in White Lion Court. What more natural than that the young men, mostly living in suburban London, enthusiastically concerned with the fortunes of Surrey or Kent or Middlesex in County matches, should dream of forming a cricket club of their own.

This was done at a meeting in White Lion Court on July 19th, 1882—the very year in which Murdoch's Australian team defeated England at the Oval and took away the legendary Ashes. Some 60 members of the staff joined at once, and Bernard Waymouth was elected President. It is of amusing, but still significant, interest that the office closing hour on Saturdays was put back from 2 p.m. to 1 p.m. on the representation of Waymouth, for the convenience of the cricketers.

The records of the club are enshrined in a volume printed for private circulation only, in 1956. In the nature of things, this is a light-hearted chronicle, highly domestic in its appeal. It makes much of all the little comedies inevitable in the running of an amateur cricket club—the search for a playing field in the crowded wilds of South London, passages with groundsmen too fond of beer and elderly horses not at all fond of work, humiliating defeats and surprising victories. However that may be, Lloyd's Register Cricket Club, approved and supported by the General Committee, came to be a formidable sodality of its kind, producing several players of County standard and at least one, W. M. Bradley, the fast bowler to play twice for England against Australia in 1899.

Senior members of the London staff were active in its affairs, both as players and administrators, and when their ladies accepted the pleasant duties of hostesses at Saturday afternoon teas, the Cricket

Club became the focal centre of a rich corporate life. Its occasional bulletin, the *Scorcher*, has a world-wide circulation, if hardly one to arouse the envy of Fleet Street. The Cricket Club Dinner was the event of the social year. It could attract 300 diners and speakers of distinction in divers fields; amid much that was frankly and properly hilarious, it might be the occasion of an important announcement from on high.

One would fain linger over some of the more entertaining aspects of the Cricket Club's development. There is, for instance, the agreeable sketch in the Club's History of Dr. Laws, "a senior and very highly academic surveyor", who was appointed captain of the Second XI in 1920. "He found it difficult to concentrate on the game and did not know his team very well, with the result that a somewhat peculiar season ensued. On one occasion he went up to his opening bowler, whom he had just rested, and, calling him by a completely different name, asked him if he would mind bowling. It was his habit to wear a white sunhat and he always fielded at point, which position appeared to have a soothing effect on him. On occasions he would appear to be almost lost to the game taking place, when a sudden cut by the batsman would rudely disturb him. As the ball sped rapidly past him he would turn, and invariably his hat came off. This was always retrieved first before he trundled after the fast disappearing leather." It is rather more remarkable, however, and oddly significant, that Andrew Scott was an even more comic performer on the field and, at the same time, the very prop and pillar of the Cricket Club over a long period of years.

This was, on the face of it, improbable. Scott was born and bred in that north-eastern county of Scotland now called Moray, and he passed his boyhood in Glasgow: neither region notable as a nursery of cricketers. He was nevertheless one of the founders of Lloyd's Register Cricket Club and followed the fortunes of the Surrey county club with passionate attention. His devotion to the lesser club was rewarded for some years during the 1890's by a sort of permanent captaincy of the Second XI, and his doings in that capacity were memorable in their oddity.

Even so, one may discern in Andrew Scott's cricketing enthusiasm a certain administrative purpose. This was almost frankly confessed in a letter he addressed to the Cricket Club Committee in

N

February, 1937, thus:—

> "Of one thing I am assured—that, whether the Club wins or loses,
> it will continue to promote a feeling of *esprit de corps* and goodwill
> amongst the different members of the staff, to the abiding advantage
> of Lloyd's Register of Shipping."

That might have suggested the perfect epitaph of this unusual and
forceful man—that what lay nearest his heart were the honour and
advancement of the Society he served so long.

Out of the Cricket Club there grew inevitably a popular Lawn
Tennis section, but there grew much more. In some of its less frivolous
passages the History of the Cricket Club shrewdly makes the point
that the younger players, most of them out of much the same social
and educational environment, were of the sort who accepted the
responsibility of the citizen to play a part in national defence.

Some readers of a younger generation may have to be reminded of
the state of the world during the first decade of the 20th Century. The
European scene was dominated by the probability of large-scale
military conflict. Great Britain felt reasonably secure behind the
sure shield of the Royal Navy. But the veteran Lord Roberts and
some others argued continually for the need of a stronger Army, even
to the point of conscription; and the movement had its satisfaction,
however much a typically British compromise it may have been, in
the creation of the Territorial Army in 1908. Without being called
upon to pronounce large judgments on historical issues, however, we
merely note here that the alarms of the period affected a large number
of precisely the type of young man employed by such institutions as
Lloyd's Register of Shipping.

To most people nowadays it must seem a triviality that, during the
two summers before the outbreak of the First World War, the
Cricket Club was often hard put to it to field a good First XI, so many
of the brighter stars attending Territorial camps, but the fact has still
its historical significance. A typical growth of the period, and out of
the Cricket Club, was the Rifle Club. It was first mooted as early as
1905 by F. A. Mayne, a stalwart in Head Office and in all the Staff's
social and sporting activities, but it did not come into existence until
1909, after the formation of the Territorial Army. The General
Committee allowed and financed the setting up of a range on the roof
of No. 71, Fenchurch Street, and an enthusiastic club was duly formed

under the Captaincy of W. J. Parsons, a Boer War veteran. Lady members of the Staff are now eligible for membership, and both its teams and individuals have distinguished themselves in competition.

The increase in the popularity of golf had its natural reflection, in 1934, in the formation of Lloyd's Register Golfing Society. With an average membership of 90, it has its own trophies for internal competition and its matches with other clubs of the kind. No occasion is more thoroughly enjoyed than the annual match between the Committee and the Staff, a happy event in which the brisk, young men among the juniors are not always triumphant over their governors.

The most recent expression of staff solidarity was the formation in 1951 of Lloyd's Register Arts Guild, for membership of which the wives of staff members are now eligible. This started from an experimental exhibition of arts and crafts held at Head Office in November, 1951, the display containing so many pictures and pieces of quality that an association was promptly formed. The Arts Guild is nowadays able to stage an exhibition every second year approximately, a fair number of entries coming from abroad, and representative selections of perhaps a hundred exhibits have been sent on tour to the larger outport offices in Glasgow, Liverpool and Newcastle.

The formation of a Staff Association in 1920 was a domestic event of real moment. If this sodality does without the convivial tradition of the Cricket Club, it is a useful medium for the circulation of specialised information among departments; an expert on, say, the Engineering side reading to his colleagues a paper on a new development that may concern them all in their daily work. One of these papers—R. J. Sladden's "Notes and Anecdotes of the Society's Staff during the Victorian Era"—has been laid under tribute in these pages, but most of the discourses are of a technical nature. They are regularly printed at Garrett House and circulated as Private and Confidential documents.

Even in the light-hearted History of the Cricket Club it is possible to perceive a connection with one of the Society's more serious concerns. The General Committee were always well disposed towards the Cricket Club, and when the latter wandered from one playing field in South London to another and came to rest at length in Gallery Road, Dulwich, the Society financed the building of the

N*

pavilion, which is also an agreeable clubhouse. But Gallery Road lies hard by Dulwich College, and there was thus set up a cordial relationship between Lloyd's Register Cricket Club and the senior boys of Alleyn's School, the venerable institution within the same foundation. The association became so close that, in brief, the Society could look to the old school for likely recruits to its administrative staff at least—especially when Andrew Scott dominated the scene, his shrewd eye at once on a likely cricketer and a young man of character and intelligence.

There is no formal way of entry into the service of Lloyd's Register of Shipping, whether on the technical or the administrative side; that is, competitive examination as for the Civil Service is not part of the system. Over a long period of years the Society offered scholarships in both naval architecture and marine engineering at the Royal Naval College, Greenwich, and at a number of British Universities. Abroad, likely recruits in the United States and Japan were encouraged by two annual subventions in each case. All these benefactions were discontinued in 1928 for a variety of reasons; and when the position was surveyed after the Second World War it was deemed that the new provisions for State scholarships and County awards had largely removed the need for encouragement from the Society direct. In their place, the Committee sponsors through the Institute of Marine Engineers an annual lecture for apprentices and covers their expenses in attending.

For the rest, recruitment for staff within the United Kingdom reflects the respect the Society has earned for itself as a great British institution with international responsibilities. During a period after the Second World War all branches felt the pressure of competition exercised by expanding industry, especially its apparently insatiable demand for graduates in Science, but that phase passed. The relatively few vacancies on the administrative side can usually be filled without difficulty in collaboration with such bodies as the Public Schools Appointments Board; the Chief Surveyors, Ship and Engineer, are at the end of a bush telegraph that, with exchanges in the largest centres of production throughout the country, passes word of likely young men who, with good degrees in Science and thorough working experience, are willing in satisfactory numbers to enter a service that has a great tradition behind it, is well-paid and decently secure, and offers to the adventurous the prospect of occasional sojourns in interesting places overseas.

"Eppur si muove . . . Nevertheless it does move," Galileo is said to have exclaimed in the face of the Inquisition that abhorred his conception of the planetary system. It moves, it works, however mysterious it may seem; and one is tempted to apply the phrase to Lloyd's Register of Shipping.

As has already been suggested, and as at least one Chairman bluntly said, the strict legal position of the Society is nearly indefinable, its constitution beautifully vague. It could fairly be described as a typically English—as distinct from British—growth: the product of a national genius for compromise on the one hand and for technical excellence on the other. The miracle is that this institution—wholly a voluntary body except in so far as its staff must be adequately rewarded—is internationally accepted as the supreme arbiter of what is true and sound and good in shipbuilding, marine engineering and in many other fields of construction besides.

This History should have made it clear that the Society is made up of acknowledged leaders in the shipping world—in shipbuilding, in the various branches of engineering, in shipowning and in underwriting. Chairmen come and go, and the composition of the General Committee reflects continually the inevitability of change. Its members are elected by their peers, in many countries abroad as in the United Kingdom; and the worn phrase about "enlightened self-interest" is simply not good enough for the existence of such a body. This continuing existence is more in the nature of a mystery, though some may find in it more practically a triumph of morality or simple decency.

Sine Præjudicio . . . That is a high claim that no individual short of saintliness could fairly make, but it is made with proper modesty in the motto adopted by the Society when a Coat-of-Arms was, in 1958, finally approved by the College of Arms.

It will be recalled that, for many years on end, the symbol associated with Lloyd's Register of Shipping was the "Lady", designed by Harry J. Cornish. The affection of the Society's members and servants for that creature of fancy will be a long time a-dying, but it was felt as the anniversary year of 1960 approached that Lloyd's Register of Shipping should at length have Arms and a Badge appropriate to its age and standing. The College of Arms passes such matters through a very fine filter of conventions and precedents, and it took the best part of two years to determine in what symbols and colours the Society's function could most appropriately be suggested.

The Arms finally approved and registered are easily read, even by the layman. Ignoring the recondite terminology of heraldry, the central point of the design is the open Register Book with a symbolic ship across the pages and, above, the heraldic device called a Mercantile Crown: the latter indicating the association with merchant shipping. The fearsome figures to left and right, technically the "supporters", are the regal beasts of sea and land, the dolphin and the lion; the dolphin bearing the Society's unique mark of classification, the lion the emblem of the sun. Above the decorative mantling over the heads of the beasts stands something like the familiar figure of the "Lady," her left hand resting on a blue anchor, the symbol of security.

These elements, however roughly described, are known to heraldry as the Shield, Wreath and Crest, the whole design as the Arms; but the equipment includes a Badge, which may be used as a cap badge, on the title pages of books, or for letter headings and the like. This is a simple arrangement of the heraldic ship on an oval red ground within a mounting of coiled ropes, the whole surmounted by the Mercantile Crown. Now, English Heraldry, as distinct from Scottish, does not recognise the motto as an integral part of the Arms, but the Society's choice, duly approved, is set out on a scroll across pictorial suggestions of the Dolphin's sea and the Lion's land.

Sine Præjudicio, it runs; Without Prejudice. This is not the bold assertion of a race of noblemen or the braggart cry of a fighting family. It is calm and modest, almost a humble statement of belief. This story has been ill told if it has not justified the claim.

INDEX

Names of Ships and Yachts are printed in italics

INDEX

INDEX

INDEX

Shipowners, Builders and Marine Engineers not included
in the General Index